STRATEGIES FOR TEACHING

Elementary and Middle-Level Chorus

Compiled and edited by
Ann R. Small and Judy K. Bowers

YOUR KEY TO IMPLEMENTING THE NATIONAL STANDARDS FOR MUSIC EDUCATION

MUSIC EDUCATORS NATIONAL CONFERENCE

MENC MENC
MENC MENC

STRATEGIES FOR TEACHING

Elementary and Middle-Level Chorus

MENC wishes to thank
Carolynn A. Lindeman for developing and coordinating this series;
Ann R. Small and *Judy K. Bowers*
for selecting, writing, and editing the strategies for this book;
and the following teachers for submitting strategies:

Patricia L. Arnett

J. Bryan Burton

Nancy Ann Cooper

Jo-Ann L. Decker-St. Pierre

Liam Dunch

Darla Eshelman

Heather Eyerly

Linda E. Ferreira

R. J. David Frego

Janet Galván

Joan E. Gregoryk

Julie Jackson

Alan C. McClung

Stephen Mulder

Emma R. Oberheuser

Melissa E. Popovich

Rebecca R. Reames

Carole M. Swope

Patricia Windemuth Banta

Dawn C. Wooderson

Susan C. Wyatt

Mark Ziegler

CONTENTS

PREFACE

The Music Educators National Conference (MENC) created the *Strategies for Teaching* series to help preservice and in-service music educators implement the K–12 National Standards for Music Education and the MENC Prekindergarten Standards. To address the many components of the school music curriculum, each book in the series focuses on a specific curricular area and a particular level. The result is eleven books spanning the K–12 areas of band, chorus, general music, strings/orchestra, guitar, keyboard, and specialized ensembles. A prekindergarten book and a guide for college music methods classes complete the series.

The purpose of the series is to seize the opportunity presented by the landmark education legislation of 1994. With the passage of the Goals 2000: Educate America Act, the arts were established for the first time in our country's history as a core, challenging subject in which all students need to demonstrate competence. Voluntary academic standards were called for in all nine of the identified core subjects—standards specifying what students need to know and be able to do when they exit grades 4, 8, and 12.

In music, content and achievement standards were drafted by an MENC task force. They were examined and commented on by music teachers across the country, and the task force reviewed their comments and refined the standards. While all students in grades K–8 are expected to meet the achievement standards specified for those levels, two levels of achievement—proficient and advanced—are designated for students in grades 9–12. Students who elect music courses for one to two years beyond grade 8 are expected to perform at the proficient level. Students who elect music courses for three to four years beyond grade 8 are expected to perform at the advanced level.

The music standards, together with the dance, theatre, and visual arts standards, were presented in final form—*National Standards for Arts Education*—to the U.S. Secretary of Education in March 1994. Recognizing the importance of early childhood education, MENC went beyond the K–12 standards and established content and achievement standards for the prekindergarten level as well, which are included in MENC's *The School Music Program: A New Vision*.

Now the challenge at hand is to implement the standards at the state and local levels. Implementation may require schools to expand the resources necessary to achieve the standards as specified in MENC's *Opportunity-to-Learn Standards for Music Instruction: Grades PreK–12.* Teachers will need to examine their curricula to determine if they lead to achievement of the standards. For many, the standards reflect exactly what has always been included in the school music curriculum—they represent best practice. For others, the standards may call for some curricular expansion.

To assist in the implementation process, this series offers teaching strategies illustrating how the music standards can be put into action in the music classroom. The strategies themselves do not suggest a curriculum. That, of course, is the responsibility of school districts and individual teachers. The strategies, however, are designed to help in curriculum development, lesson planning, and assessment of music learning.

The teaching strategies are based on the content and achievement standards specified in the *National Standards for Arts Education* (K–12) and *The School Music Program: A New Vision* (PreK–12). Although the strategies, like the standards, are designed primarily for four-year-olds, fourth graders, eighth graders, and high school seniors, many may be developmentally appropriate for students in other grades. Each strategy, a lesson appropriate for a portion of a class session or a complete class session, includes an objective (a clear statement of what the student will be able to do), a list of necessary materials, a description of what prior student learning and experiences are expected, a set of procedures, and the indicators of success. A follow-up section identifies ways learning may be expanded.

The *Guide for Music Methods Classes* contains strategies appropriate for preservice instructional settings in choral, instrumental, and general music methods classes. The teaching strategies in this guide relate to the other books in the series and reflect a variety of teaching/learning styles.

Bringing a series of thirteen books from vision to reality required tremendous commitment from many, many music educators—not to mention the tireless help of the MENC publications staff. Literally hundreds of music teachers across the country answered the call to participate in this project, the largest such participation in an MENC publishing endeavor. The contributions of these teachers and the books' editors are proudly presented in the various publications.

—Carolynn A. Lindeman
Series Editor

---

*Carolynn A. Lindeman, professor of music at San Francisco State University and president of the Music Educators National Conference (1996–1998), served on the MENC task force that developed the music education standards. She is the author of three college textbooks (*The Musical Classroom, PianoLab, *and* MusicLab) *and numerous articles.*

INTRODUCTION

Music educators have always believed in teaching children to sing well. Children are not only capable of singing well, but also of rendering extremely artistic performances of great choral music.

Choral singing is a *performing* art. In music education, we continue to discover that children often can perform what they cannot always verbalize. These choral strategies, therefore, are based primarily on the performance of singing. In most of the strategies, the authors offer musical challenges that require students to demonstrate learning during or after performance. They ask students to make musical decisions, to reflect on their learning, and to demonstrate discovery through performance, regardless of whether these students have the vocabulary to verbalize their ideas fully. Collectively, the strategies illustrate the premise that children have extraordinary capacity to make associations, form assumptions, and draw conclusions when the teacher structures the language of music into musical examples, questions, and choices that require musical decision making. As their cognitive development and verbal knowledge increase, students learn to verbalize their concepts.

The authors of these strategies place little value on choral methodologies that include extensive explaining and lecturing. Current research in education recognizes many forms of thinking and knowing, including musical thinking, which is apparent in the acts of singing, playing, and composing. The manifestation of musical thinking, apart from verbal expression, will be expressed occasionally in these strategies as "singing one's knowledge." Singing is, in itself, a form of musical thinking. These choral strategies require students in kindergarten through grade 8 to "sing, improvise, compose, move, and play" their musical understanding, as well as use musical vocabulary to talk about what they know.

There are many different choral pieces used in these strategies; all of the songs are exemplary in their style or genre. The approaches to teaching are many and varied. Some strategies contain specific suggestions of materials and sequenced activities. Others provide a structure that allows the teacher to fill in some details of sequence and use materials of choice.

This collection is written for professional music teachers. Most of them will read and study it for ideas. As they read, they will mentally adapt the ideas it contains to personal teaching situations. They will note that most of the strategies will work with different pieces, or with easier or more difficult rhythm patterns, or other improvisation materials. Although most strategies are directed toward the exit levels (fourth and eighth grades) as described in the National Standards for Music Education, there are some strategies for younger students. Master teachers will identify processes behind the strategies that could work in a number of contexts. It would be unfortunate for a teacher to cast the volume aside because there is no budget for choral octavos, or because he or she does not like the suggested songs or the particular sequence of activities. These strategies are innovative and flexible; they can work in many variations. Although many of the strategies are designed for a portion of a class session or even an entire class session, some of them contain challenges that will require more than one class or rehearsal period for full exploration. The resource list is valuable for new teachers as well as those who have considerable experience.

The editors and authors of these choral strategies are enthusiastic about the future of choral music education. We offer this book with all good wishes that it will mark a significant journey toward music learning, excellence, and a rich experience in the choral art.

STRATEGIES
Grades K–4

STANDARD 1A

Singing, alone and with others, a varied repertoire of music: Students sing independently, on pitch and in rhythm, with appropriate timbre, diction, and posture, and maintain a steady tempo.

Objective

- Students will sing a call-and-response song independently and chorally with accurate pitches, clear diction, good tone quality, and appropriate dynamics and timbre, while maintaining a steady tempo.

Materials

- "Oliver Cromwell," arr. Benjamin Britten (New York: Boosey & Hawkes), OCTB5893, unison, Level 1—also in *We Will Sing*, by Doreen Rao (New York: Boosey & Hawkes, 1993)
- Chalkboard, or chart, with notated rhythm and pitches (but not text) of the phrase "Hee, haw, buried and dead," from "Oliver Cromwell"

Prior Knowledge and Experiences

- Students can sing the basic solfège scale and use the Curwen hand signs for high *do, sol, fa, mi,* and low *do*.

Procedures

1. Using hand signs for the pitches high *do, sol, fa, mi,* and low *do,* improvise two-measure phrases in 6/8 rhythm and have students sing and sign them back to you. Present different rhythm patterns using these pitches, initially at slow to moderate tempos. Ask students to raise their hands when they sing the phrase notated on the chalkboard or chart. Gradually work into the melodic and rhythmic pattern in the phrase "Hee, haw, buried and dead." Echo-sing that phrase using syllables in a variety of keys, ending in E-flat major. Ask students to echo the phrase several times using syllables and hand signs.

2. As students look at the score, ask, "On what words do you find the phrase we sang?" Sing the phrase again, using syllables to remind them. [*Note:* In this strategy, the phrases of the song "Oliver Cromwell" are treated as calls and responses. Responses include "Hee, haw, buried and dead," "Hee, haw, over his head," "Hee, haw, ready to fall," etc. The text immediately preceding each response is considered a call. Since the pitches are the same for all the phrases in the song, students may confuse the rhythms of some of the calls with the rhythm of the response.]

3. After students discover that the phrase is "Hee, haw, buried and dead," sing it with text and, as the students echo, point to the notation. Challenge students to find the other places in the music that are like "Hee, haw, buried and dead" (such as "Hee, haw, over his head" and "Hee, haw, ready to fall"). Have students echo-sing all these phrases using texts.

4. Now sing the calls and let students sing the responses using the texts. After the group sings the responses, call on volunteers to sing the responses individually. Give more than one chance if the pitches are not correct the first time, slowing the tempo to facilitate accuracy.

(continued)

5. Continue the call-response activity using correct dynamics and in styles appropriate to the texts throughout the song. Experiment with different vocal timbres as the text changes; for example, "There came an old woman to gather them all" may call for a more nasal, pinched sound. Invite individual volunteers to sing the calls and responses in vocal timbres or styles they think best fit the texts. Correct any incorrect pitches and insist on good breath support enhanced by correct posture. Be sure that students keep a steady beat throughout the piece.

6. For the last performance of the song, let students choose the best style or timbre to use for various portions of the text while not overdoing unusual tone qualities. After reminding students to use correct dynamics, good diction, and proper breath support, conduct a performance of the whole song, maintaining a steady beat.

Indicators of Success

- Students sing on pitch, with good posture, breath support, tone quality, and diction.
- Students use appropriate dynamics and timbre with various stanzas and keep a steady beat.

Follow-up

- During students' early choral experiences, introduce strophic art songs containing appropriate texts, pitch ranges, and tessituras for them; for example, "Die Forelle" ("The Trout") or "Das Wandern" ("Wandering") by Franz Schubert. These works offer opportunities to address dynamics, blend, style or timbre, and rhythmic variety without requiring students to spend an inordinate amount of time learning pitches.

STANDARD 1B

Singing, alone and with others, a varied repertoire of music: Students sing expressively, with appropriate dynamics, phrasing, and interpretation.

Objective

- Students will sing a familiar song on pitch, rhythmically, and with good phrasing and dynamics.

Materials

- "America" ("My country, 'tis of thee"), in *The Music Connection,* Grades K–4 (Parsippany, NJ: Silver Burdett Ginn, 1995); *Share the Music,* Grades 1–4 (New York: Macmillan/McGraw-Hill, 1995); *Music and You,* Grades K–3 (New York: Macmillan/McGraw-Hill, 1991); or *World of Music,* Grades K–4 (Parsippany, NJ: Silver Burdett Ginn, 1991)

- Audiocassette recorder, microphone, and blank tape

Prior Knowledge and Experiences

- Students can sing "America" from memory.

Procedures

[*Note:* Students often sing "America" giving equal stress to all notes and text syllables. A slightly waltz-like treatment of the rhythm will be conducive to a more musical performance of the song.]

1. With students, chant "1-2-3, 1-2-3," *lightly* emphasizing the first beat. Have students continue to count, lightly patsching on 1. Echo-chant the text phrase by phrase in the correct rhythm, slightly accenting beat 1.

2. Echo-sing by phrases: "My country, 'tis of thee, Sweet land of liberty," [*breath*] "Of thee I sing." Start singing softly, crescendo to *forte* on "Sweet land of liberty," and decrescendo to *piano* on "Of thee I sing." Do not breathe between "thee" and "Sweet."

3. Echo-sing by phrases: "Land where my fathers died, Land of the pilgrims' pride," [*breath*] "From every mountainside, Let freedom ring." Do not breathe between "died" and "Land" or between "mountainside" and "Let." Start the dynamics at *mezzo forte* and crescendo to *forte* on "From every mountainside." Round off the phrase by softening to *mezzo piano* on "Let freedom ring."

4. Conduct the students through the song, listening carefully to be sure that they are *lightly* emphasizing beat 1. Check pitch-matching.

5. As you conduct the song, make your conducting gestures communicate dynamics and phrasing. Pay close attention to the students' dynamics. Ask, "Do we sing the entire song loudly? Do we sing the entire song softly? Are there times when we sing more loudly than other times? On what words do we sing loudest? On what words do we sing softly?"

6. Ask students to listen while you sing the song again and to tell you the words where you carry the phrase over without breathing. Model the song again using correct dynamics and phrasing and lightly emphasizing the first beat of each measure.

7. Conduct students through the song once or twice more. Record their final performance. Play the recording so that students can hear whether they sang on pitch, used correct dynamics, and did not breathe between "thee" and "Sweet," "died" and "Land," "mountainside" and "Let."

(continued)

Indicators of Success

- Students sing more musically as a result of singing rhythmically, using a variety of dynamic levels, and phrasing correctly (taking breaths and carrying the phrase over in appropriate places in the text).
- Students improve in their ability to match pitches over time.

Follow-up

- Have students breathe properly in appropriate places in other songs. Encourage students to be aware of dynamics in these new works.
- Since pitch-matching accuracy tends to improve with focused practice, have students attend to pitch-matching in all the songs they sing.

STANDARD 1C

Singing, alone and with others, a varied repertoire of music: Students sing from memory a varied repertoire of songs representing genres and styles from diverse cultures.

Objective

- Students will perform a Maori hymn from memory using appropriate body movement and singing style.

Materials

- "Tama Ngakau Marie," traditional Maori hymn, easy (see figure)

Prior Knowledge and Experiences

- Students can find Polynesia on a globe or map and have been given background information about New Zealand and one of its indigenous peoples, the Maori.

- Students have listened to and sung rhythm patterns of Hawaiian music and have sung Hawaiian songs.

- Students have been learning the melody and words to "Tama Ngakau Marie."

Procedures

1. Review "Tama Ngakau Marie" (melody and words together) by singing one phrase at a time, if necessary for reinforcement. Tell students that in the Maori culture songs are learned by imitating a leader and explaining the meaning of the text.

2. Have students perform the song sitting in their normal seating arrangement with no written music to prompt them. Any comfortable key is fine; usually this will be between D and G.

3. Ask students to clear a space where they can stand in rows with the girls at the front and the boys at the back. (For greater authenticity, have students remove their shoes.) Have students follow your example as you move slowly from right to left foot, right–close, left–close, to the quarter-note beat, which equals one measure. It is natural to have a slight swing to the body along with the steps, which encourages the gentle duple feeling of the music.

4. After you or a student has given the initial pitch, sing the song, with body movement, as a group. [*Note:* In an authentic performance, no opening pitch is given, one person sings the first line, and the chorus joins on the second line.]

Indicators of Success

- Students accurately perform "Tama Ngakau Marie" from memory with appropriate movement and accurate pronunciation.

Follow-up

- Have students experiment with improvising homophonic (for authenticity) harmonies to this melody.

(continued)

- Use "Tama Ngakau Marie" as a three-chord guitar song students play in the key of D; or transpose the melody and chord symbols to the key of G. If guitarists are used, have them stand behind the boys in the group during the performance.

Tama Ngakau Marie

Traditional Maori song
Arr. Julie J. Jackson

With gentle swing (♩ = 60)

Ta- ma nga-kau Ma- ri- e   Ta- ma a te a- tu- a

Te- nei to- nu ma- tou   a - ro- hai- na   mai.

Translation: Son of Mary, Son of God, Here we all are, Love us.

STANDARD 1D

Singing, alone and with others, a varied repertoire of music:
Students sing ostinatos, partner songs, and rounds.

Objective

- Students will sing partner songs in tune, selecting chord patterns to accompany the melodies and stating why partner songs can be sung simultaneously.

Materials

- "When the Saints Go Marching In" (written in or transposed to the key of G), in *The Music Connection*, Grade 1 (Parsippany, NJ: Silver Burdett Ginn, 1995); *Share the Music*, Grade 5 (New York: Macmillan/ McGraw-Hill, 1995); *Music and You*, Grade 5 (New York: Macmillan/McGraw-Hill, 1991); or *World of Music*, Grades 1 and 5 (Parsippany, NJ: Silver Burdett Ginn, 1991)

- "Good Night, Ladies" (written in or transposed to the key of G), in *World of Music*, Grade 6

- Another song (such as "It's a Small World," in *Music and You*, Grade 4, written in or transposed to the key of G) that does not fit harmonically with these partner songs

- Baritone ukeleles, chorded zithers (such as Autoharps or ChromAharps), or guitars, all tuned together

Procedures

1. Have students sing "When the Saints Go Marching In" a cappella. Immediately afterward, have selected students strum the following pattern in 4/4 (each chord letter corresponding to a quarter-note beat).

   G G G G / G G G G / G G G G / D7 D7 D7 D7

   G G G G / C C C C / G G D7 D7 / G G G ⁊

   Pattern A

2. Challenge students to sing "When the Saints Go Marching In" with the instrumental accompaniment of Pattern A. (Have them sing "Oh when the" as a pickup to beat one and sing "Saints" on beat one with the first chord.)

3. Ask students to sing "Good Night, Ladies" a cappella. Then have them try "Good Night, Ladies" with the instrumental accompaniment of Pattern A. (Have them sing "Good" on beat one with the first chord and give "Good" and "night" two beats each; give "-dies" three beats.)

4. Ask students to sing "It's a Small World" (or another selected song) a cappella. Have them try to sing it with the Pattern A accompaniment. Ask, "Does this song fit the chords well as they are?" [*No.*] Have students try the song with the following accompaniment, singing "It's a" as a pickup to beat one and singing "World" on the first strum of the pattern.

   G G G G / D7 D7 D7 D7 / D7 D7 D7 D7 / G G G G

   G G G G / C C C C / D7 D7 D7 D7 / G G G ⁊

   Pattern B

   Ask students whether the song fits this pattern. [*Yes.*]

5. Challenge students to try the other two songs with Pattern B. Ask whether they fit the pattern. [*No.*] Ask students: "Of the three songs, which two are 'partners'? Why are 'When the Saints' and 'Good Night, Ladies' partners?" [*The same harmonic pattern (or accompaniment) fits both songs.*]

(continued)

- Chalkboard, or chart, showing chord patterns of the songs listed

Prior Knowledge and Experiences

- Students can sing accurately "When the Saints Go Marching In," "Good Night, Ladies," and the other selected song.
- Students can play I, IV, and V7 chords in the key of G on baritone ukeleles, Autoharps/ ChromAharps, and guitars.

6. Have students perform the partner songs together with no accompaniment, staying in tune and keeping a steady beat.

7. Conduct students through a final performance of the partner songs with instrumental accompaniment, having them first perform each song alone and then perform them together.

Indicators of Success

- Students identify the correct partner songs and explain why partner songs can be sung together.
- Students show discomfort when chords do not fit the harmony of the melody, and they express satisfaction when correct harmonies are played.
- Students sing the partner songs together, in tune, with and without accompaniment.

Follow-up

- Have students compile a list of I-V7 or I-IV-V7 songs from their basal series music textbook. Identify for students the letter names of the notes in the I, IV, and V7 chords in various keys, and let them figure out the harmonic patterns of various songs on their list, looking for two songs that could be partners.

STANDARD 1E

Singing, alone and with others, a varied repertoire of music: Students sing in groups, blending vocal timbres, matching dynamic levels, and responding to the cues of a conductor.

Objective

- Students will perform a song in unison and as a two-part round, following conductor cues as to tempo, dynamics, attacks, and releases, and singing on pitch and blending with the ensemble.

Materials

- "Haida" (Hebrew folk song), arr. Henry Leck (Fort Lauderdale, FL: Plymouth Music Company), HL-516, unison and round, Level 1

Prior Knowledge and Experiences

- Students can match pitches.
- Students have experience watching a conductor for directions.

Procedures

1. Teach "Haida" by modeling and having students echo-sing. At first, model the entire vocal line, indicating where the claps come. Then have the chorus join in on the claps.

2. On both the A and B sections of the song, chant the words in rhythm by phrases—"Hai-da, hai-da, hai-di-di-dai-da, . . ."—and have students imitate in rhythm so that they will quickly grasp the song.

3. As the song increases in tempo, caution students to blend their singing voices rather than shout. Ask, "What do you think 'blend your voices' means?" Teach blending by using an example and a nonexample. Perhaps have three students sing a portion of the song, having secretly asked one to sing louder than the other two. Then have them sing while listening to one another so that none of the three is heard above the others. Challenge listeners to identify the example in which the singers blended their voices.

4. When students can sing the piece well, divide the class into two parts and challenge them to perform the piece as a round.

5. Have students follow the directions for movement suggested in the piece.

6. Rehearse tempo changes and releases in short segments until all students are watching and can follow you precisely. [*Note:* There are sections that speed up and slow down, that end abruptly, or that are held until a definite release.]

7. Remind students to watch you closely and follow your cues for tempo indications, dynamic directions, attacks, and releases. Have students perform the piece.

Indicators of Success

- Students perform the piece together successfully, singing in unison and in a two-part round with movement, blending their voices, and performing at correct dynamic levels.

- On cue from the conductor, students gradually increase the tempo as a group, sustain held notes, and release the sound together.

(continued)

Follow-up

- Introduce students to other pieces that demand focused attention on the conductor for clean attacks and releases, accurate tempo, and precise dynamic changes; for example, "Ching-a-Ring Chaw," arr. Aaron Copland (New York: Boosey & Hawkes), OCTB6609, unison, Level 2—also in *We Will Sing* by Doreen Rao (New York: Boosey & Hawkes, 1993); and "The Birds" by Benjamin Britten (New York: Boosey & Hawkes), OCTB6524, unison, Level 1.

STANDARD 2A

Performing on instruments, alone and with others, a varied repertoire of music: Students perform on pitch, in rhythm, with appropriate dynamics and timbre, and maintain a steady tempo.

Objective

- Students will perform with appropriate dynamics and timbre the accompaniment to a song from their repertoire using nonpitched percussion instruments.

Materials

- Piece from the group's choral repertoire (such as folk or popular song) with clear, regular rhythms
- Variety of nonpitched percussion instruments

Prior Knowledge and Experiences

- Students have sung and performed simple songs.
- Students understand the concept of beat.
- Students have performed simple rhythm patterns in echo games.
- Students have learned the names of and correct method of holding and playing various nonpitched percussion instruments.

Procedures

1. Have students sing through the selected song.
2. Review the concept of beat, and have students clap the beat as they sing the song. Clap the rhythm patterns of the song and have students echo them.
3. Present simple ostinatos for the song, aurally or with notation, depending on the level of the group.
4. Ask students to read and clap (or echo) the ostinatos.
5. Have students discuss possible timbres for the different accompaniment patterns. Then distribute the instruments to students.
6. Rehearse the ostinatos, adding a dynamics scheme for phrases that are identical.
7. Have students perform the song. After a successful performance, have students switch parts, switch between singing and playing, or both.

Indicators of Success

- Students accurately perform learned accompaniment patterns for the selected song with appropriate dynamics and timbre and with a steady tempo.

Follow-up

- Have students learn to use nonpitched percussion instruments to accompany other songs in their repertoire that feature distinct forms (such as ABACA) and exhibit contrast.
- Have students try using some pitched percussion instruments to accompany songs from their repertoire.

STANDARD 2B

Performing on instruments, alone and with others, a varied repertoire of music:
Students perform easy rhythmic, melodic, and chordal patterns accurately and
independently on rhythmic, melodic, and harmonic classroom instruments.

Objective

- Students will accompany accurately and independently a folk song using recorder and Orff mallet instruments or resonator bells.

Materials

- French folk song "Fais dodo" (written in or transposed to the key of G), in *The Music Connection,* Grade 5 (Parsippany, NJ: Silver Burdett Ginn, 1995)
- Recorders
- Orff mallet instruments or resonator bells arranged in G pentatonic
- Finger cymbals or soprano glockenspiel

Prior Knowledge and Experiences

- Students have played Orff mallet instruments or resonator bells, and finger cymbals or soprano glockenspiel.
- Students can play the pitches B, A, G on the recorder.
- Students are familiar with "layering technique" for voices and instruments.
- Students have experience using the solfège syllables *mi, re,* and *do.*

Procedures

1. After explaining that "fais dodo" is a French expression meaning "take a nap," which parents say to sleepy children, have students echo the song "Fais dodo" line by line in the key of G. Then have students sing the melody with letter names (B, A, G).

2. Have students play the melody on the recorder, first echoing each phrase to review fingerings and then playing the entire song. Have part of the class sing with letter names while the other students play the melody on their recorders.

3. Teach the phrase "Close your eyes and sleep now my brother," patsching on the downbeat—the words "close" and "sleep." Have students play this rhythm on a bass metallophone or resonator bells, repeatedly playing an open G-D chord on the words "close" and "sleep." Add this accompaniment to the melody.

4. Have students create a second instrumental part in 3/4 meter, starting with the following repeated phrase:

    Have students patsch the rhythm using alternating hands. Then have them transfer this rhythm pattern to an alto xylophone or resonator bells on pitches G, G, D, B, G, and add this to the melody and bass accompaniment.

5. Ask students to practice saying and patsching the following simple repeated phrase:

    $$\frac{3}{4} \quad \text{ } \quad \text{Nap} \quad \text{time}$$

    Then have them transfer the rhythm to finger cymbals or a soprano glockenspiel on a repeated D. Add the phrase to the ensemble.

6. Have students layer voices, recorders, and other instruments in various combinations to create a final composition.

Indicators of Success

- Using recorder and other classroom instruments, students sing and accompany the folk song with accurate pitches and rhythms.

Follow-up

- Have students perform the final composition for another class or in a concert setting.

- Have students, as a class, create and perform new accompaniments to "Fais dodo" and other songs in their repertoire.

STANDARD 2C

Performing on instruments, alone and with others, a varied repertoire of music: Students perform expressively a varied repertoire of music representing diverse genres and styles.

Objective

- Students will accompany American folk songs on the Autoharp/ChromAharp using D and A7 chords.

Materials

- "Shoo, Fly" (written in or transposed to the key of D), in *The Music Connection*, Grade 5 (Parsippany, NJ: Silver Burdett Ginn, 1995); *Share the Music*, Grade 2 (New York: Macmillan/ McGraw-Hill, 1995); *Music and You*, Grade 2 (New York: Macmillan/McGraw-Hill, 1991); or *World of Music*, Grades 2 and 5 (Parsippany, NJ: Silver Burdett Ginn, 1991)
- Chord notation for "Shoo, Fly" in the key of D (for students able to hear chord changes)
- Chorded zither (such as Autoharp or ChromAharp)

Prior Knowledge and Experiences

- Students can sing simple unison songs with teacher accompanying on Autoharp/ChromAharp.

Procedures

1. Introduce "Shoo, Fly" by singing the chorus while accompanying yourself on the Autoharp/ChromAharp using D and A7 chords. Use a relaxed tempo to demonstrate the syncopation.

2. Teach students the chorus and verses, unaccompanied by rote.

3. Demonstrate how the Autoharp/ChromAharp can be held in the performer's lap and played as follows: The left hand presses a chord button, in this case D or A7, and the right hand crosses over to strum. Use thumb, fingernail of index finger, or soft or hard pick, to strum the basic stroke, an "upstroke" that begins near the performer's body (the low strings) and moves outward across the high strings. Vary the upstroke by shortening the length and playing in different octaves.

4. After your demonstration, ask students to imitate the strumming motion as they sing the song.

5. Invite individual students to play the Autoharp/ChromAharp, strumming the same chord until cued by another student or students to change chords as the class sings the song.

6. Invite individual students to practice accompanying the song on the Autoharp/ChromAharp. Add voices to the accompaniment. To keep the song interesting, elicit new rhyming words for the verses and encourage singers to improvise body percussion ostinatos during the chorus section.

7. Review a previously learned simple song that uses two chords, such as "Polly Wolly Doodle" or "Skip to My Lou." Solicit new volunteers to accompany these songs on the instrument.

Indicators of Success

- Students accurately accompany two-chord songs on the Autoharp/ChromAharp.

Follow-up

- Have students expand their accompanying skills on Autoharp/ChromAharp to include different strumming techniques, three-chord songs, and transposition of two-chord songs into other keys.

STANDARD 2D

Performing on instruments, alone and with others, a varied repertoire of music:
Students echo short rhythms and melodic patterns.

Objective

- Students will echo short rhythm patterns on classroom instruments, demonstrate visualization of the melodic contour, and reproduce melodic sequences.

Materials

- Pitched classroom instruments, including glockenspiels, metallophones, and xylophones
- Rope cut into one-yard lengths (one for every two students)
- Lummi sticks or chopsticks
- Keyboard

Prior Knowledge and Experiences

- Students can follow a leader and can sing and play various classroom instruments with a group.
- Students are familiar with proper mallet techniques and have played various pitched classroom percussion instruments.

Procedures

1. Ask half the students in the class to sit in front of pitched classroom instruments with the proper bars to create a C pentatonic scale. Pair the remaining students and seat them so that they are facing each other and each pair is tautly holding a one-yard length of rope in their left hands. Tell students who have the ropes that the length of the rope equals one measure of music.

2. At the keyboard, improvise one measure of music in 4/4 meter in C pentatonic. Ask students who are at the classroom instruments to echo the rhythm, playing any of the pitches in C pentatonic. Have students who are holding the ropes in their left hands take turns echoing the rhythm silently by tapping a right-hand finger along the length of rope from left to right. After students have had sufficient chances to try this exercise, switch the groups.

3. Again, divide students into two groups: Seat one group at the pitched instruments, and have the other group face the instrumentalists. Each student in the second group should have one lummi stick or chopstick in his or her dominant hand.

4. Play a one-measure melody in C pentatonic on the keyboard, but avoid playing on the last eighth note of the measure, thus allowing students to begin echoing on the first beat. Have students at the pitched instruments play the same melody and students with lummi sticks or chopsticks contour the melody in the air from left to right. After all students in each group have had a few chances, switch groups.

5. Once students have gained proficiency in this exercise, extend the sequence to include two measures at a time.

Indicators of Success

- Students echo short rhythmic patterns on classroom instruments.
- Students demonstrate visualization of the melodic contour.
- Students reproduce melodic sequences on classroom instruments.

(continued)

Follow-up

- To give students further opportunity to develop skill in echoing rhythmic and melodic patterns, teach them the song "Ballet of the Wind," by Grace C. Nash, in *Music with Children,* Series III, IV and More, Swartwout Productions (703 Manzanita Drive, Sedona, AZ, 86336), 1988.

STANDARD 2E

Performing on instruments, alone and with others, a varied repertoire of music: Students perform in groups, blending instrumental timbres, matching dynamic levels, and responding to the cues of a conductor.

Objective

- Students will achieve a blend of instrumental timbres, match and blend dynamic levels, and correctly respond to the cues of a student conductor.

Materials

- Classroom instruments including glockenspiels, metallophones, and xylophones, timpani, claves, maracas, wood blocks, temple blocks, conga drum, tambourines, triangles, gong, rhythm sticks, sand blocks, *cabaça*, and castanets
- Conductor's baton

Prior Knowledge and Experiences

- Students have experience singing simple songs in unison.
- Using classroom instruments, students have experience improvising eight-measure sequences over a given rhythmic ostinato.
- Students can group pitched and nonpitched percussion instruments (that is, bells, woods, and metals)
- Students have experience keeping time and indicating dynamic levels with a baton.

Procedures

1. Divide students into six groups (three for pitched percussion instruments in C pentatonic: xylophones, glockenspiels, and metallophones; and three for nonpitched percussion instruments: bells, wooden-sounding instruments, and metallic-sounding instruments). Select a student to conduct the ensemble.

2. Choose the tempo and an eight-measure rhythmic ostinato, and demonstrate it from the keyboard. The groups at nonpitched percussion instruments will play the ostinato, and the groups at pitched percussion instruments will improvise melodically and rhythmically across the eight measures. Have the student conductor indicate nonverbally which group or combination of groups will perform and the dynamics of the phrase. During the improvisatory session, support the ensemble with an accompaniment of open fifth bordun. At the end of every eight-measure phrase, have the student conductor signal a new group or combination of instruments to perform.

3. At the end of the student conductor's session, lead the group in a discussion of blending of instruments and of which combination of instruments was most successful. Have students suggest ways to improve the blend and dynamics.

4. Choose a new student conductor, have students exchange instruments, and repeat steps 2 and 3.

Indicators of Success

- Playing simple eight-measure patterns, students blend instrumental timbres, match and blend dynamic levels, and respond to the cues of student conductors.

Follow-up

- Have students increase their skill at blending instrumental timbres and dynamic levels by using instruments and singing "Solomon Grundy," arr. Grace C. Nash, in *Music with Children,* Series III, IV and More, Swartwout Productions (703 Manzanita Dr., Sedona, AZ 86336), 1988, a song that requires repetition and lends itself well to changes in dynamic level.

STANDARD 2F

Performing on instruments, alone and with others, a varied repertoire of music: Students perform independent instrumental parts while other students sing or play contrasting parts.

Objective

- Students will accompany class singing by playing various ostinatos on pitched and non-pitched classroom percussion instruments.

Materials

- "Frog Went A-Courtin'," in *Share the Music,* Grade 3 (New York: Macmillan/McGraw-Hill, 1995)
- Various Orff mallet instruments
- Various nonpitched classroom percussion instruments
- Teacher-generated rhythmic and pentatonic melodic patterns

Prior Knowledge and Experiences

- Students have sung simple folk songs as a class.
- Students have experience playing various pitched and non-pitched classroom percussion instruments.
- Students have experience imitating rhythm patterns.
- Students can clap, tap, walk, or play an ostinato in a group while another group is singing or speaking.

Procedures

1. Teach students the first verse of "Frog Went A-Courtin'," phrase by phrase, by echo-singing.
2. Using simple rhythms (quarter-note and eighth-note combinations), have half the students in the class tap a given four-count ostinato while the remaining students sing the first verse. Have students switch parts and repeat the pattern, changing the pattern when appropriate to incorporate several different ostinatos.
3. Placing as many students as possible at instruments, have the group of students playing each set of instruments (for example, xylophones, rhythm sticks, triangles) select a teacher-generated four-count ostinato or compose a new one to accompany the class.
4. Have students at the instruments play their ostinatos while the class sings "Frog Went A-Courtin'."

Indicators of Success

- Students maintain their ostinatos and keep a steady beat throughout the song.

Follow-up

- Have students perform rhythmic and melodic ostinatos to accompany other pentatonic songs.
- Over time, have students compose and perform longer and more complex ostinatos to accompany pentatonic songs.

STANDARD 3A

Improvising melodies, variations, and accompaniments: Students improvise "answers" in the same style to given rhythmic and melodic phrases.

Objective

■ Students will improvise different phrase endings for a known song and will recognize the original versions of the endings.

Materials

■ "America" ("My country, 'tis of thee"), in *The Music Connection,* Grades K–4 (Parsippany, NJ: Silver Burdett Ginn, 1995); *Share the Music,* Grades 1–4 (New York: Macmillan/McGraw-Hill, 1995); Grades K–3 (New York: Macmillan/McGraw-Hill, 1991); or *World of Music,* Grades K–4 (Parsippany, NJ: Silver Burdett Ginn, 1991)

■ Six resonator bells or choirchimes, tuned to C an octave above middle C and to D, E♭, F, G, and A in the octave beginning with middle C

Prior Knowledge and Experiences

■ Students can sing "America" from memory.

■ Students have experience following simple conducting cues indicating that they should begin or stop singing.

Procedures

1. Sing the song "America" with the students. After sufficient review, sing the song alone up to the words "Of thee I sing." At that point, ask students to sing "Of thee I sing." Starting from "Land where my fathers died," ask students to complete the song as you conduct them.

2. Sing the song up to "Of thee I sing," and then direct students to sing that part of the phrase. Continue to sing the song alone up to the word "mountainside." Then have students sing the phrase "Let freedom ring."

3. Distribute appropriate resonator bells or choirchimes (D, E♭, and F) to three students to play on the phrase "Of thee I sing" as the others sing it. Have students figure out which of them will have to play his or her note twice. Have students with bells or chimes stand in this order: D on left (1), E♭ in center (2), and F on right (3); and play in this order: 3-2-1-2. Ask students to sing the song through to that point, and have the bells or chimes playing as students sing "Of thee I sing."

4. Have students who are holding the bells or chimes rearrange themselves, or have one student rearrange the players, but ask students with bells or chimes to still play in the order they are standing (3-2-1-2). When the students get to "Of thee I sing," stop the singing and let the bells or chimes play in the rhythm of the phrase "Of thee I sing." After the bells or chimes play, have students sing the words on the pitches that were played in the new sequence. Ask whether the phrase sounds the same as or different from the way they sang it first.

5. Let other students play the bells or chimes. Choose another student to rearrange the players, but still use the 3-2-1-2 playing order; stop at the phrase "Of thee I sing" again, let the bells or chimes play in the rhythm of the phrase, and then have students sing the pitches in the new order. Change the order and players several times. Each time, have students sing the phrase in the new sequence of pitches. Finally, challenge students to remember the original pitch sequence of the phrase and rearrange the bells or chimes in the original order by listening to the sounds of the pitches.

(continued)

6. Extend the activity to the final phrase "Let freedom ring," using five students on bells or chimes (E♭, F, G, A, and C).

7. Conduct the singers as they sing the song all the way through, with bells or chimes accompanying the final phrase of each section of the song.

Indicators of Success

- Students improvise different phrase endings to the song by rearranging resonator bells or choirchimes.

- Students sing the improvised phrase endings.

- Students demonstrate that they recognize the original phrase endings by putting the bells or chimes back in the correct order and singing the pitches correctly.

Follow-up

- Have students use resonator bells or choirchimes to improvise endings to familiar songs such as "Happy Birthday."

- Arrange tones on pitched classroom instruments in a pentatonic scale. Give students a four-measure rhythm in 2/4 meter, improvise a melodic "question," and have them play an improvised "answer" in the rhythm you model.

Improvising melodies, variations, and accompaniments: Students improvise simple rhythmic and melodic ostinato accompaniments.

Objective

- Students will improvise parts of ostinato accompaniments to a simple unison song on Orff instruments using tones of the pentatonic scale.

Materials

- "Columbus Sailed with Three Ships," in *Music and You,* Grades K and 1 (New York: Macmillan/McGraw-Hill, 1991)

- Orff instruments in F pentatonic, such as xylophones or metallophones, glockenspiels, and nonpitched percussion instruments

- Two-measure ostinatos for bass and alto xylophone (or metallophone), with measures 7 and 8 blank (see steps 2–4) and measures 17 and 18 blank (see steps 2 and 6)

For example:

Bass xylophone

Alto xylophone

Procedures

1. Teach or review "Columbus Sailed with Three Ships," reminding students to sing with good posture, breath, and tone quality. If you are introducing the song, echo-sing the phrases. Correct any incorrect pitches or words.

2. When the class can sing the song all the way through, using body percussion, teach all students the ostinato for the bass xylophone, which will later be transferred to the instrument. Teach in this sequence: (a) patsch rhythm; (b) patsch rhythm and speak text; (c) patsch rhythm and sing text; (d) transfer body percussion to instruments. When you come to measures 7 and 8 ("Over the ocean blue"), clap or snap a different, but simple, rhythm, changing it every time you repeat the A section of the song. In measures 17 and 18, improvise body percussion, as you did in measures 7 and 8.

3. Have students sing the song from the beginning, patsching the bass xylophone part. At measures 7 and 8, ask students to make up their own body percussion; for example:

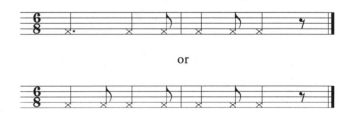

or

[*Note:* Give examples that are simple but rhythmic.] Repeat this step two times or more.

4. Send some students to bass xylophone and have them play the two-measure ostinato up to measures 7 and 8; from there, have them play either an improvisation that they created in body percussion in step 3 or a two-measure improvisation using an appropriate rhythm pattern they devise.

5. Teach the ostinato for the alto xylophone in the same sequence to everyone first. Then send players to the alto xylophones. Again have students play whatever they choose on pentatonic tones using an appropriate rhythm pattern at measures 7 and 8.

(continued)

Prior Knowledge and Experiences

- Students have sung "Columbus Sailed with Three Ships," or have the capacity to learn new songs quickly.

- Students can keep a steady beat.

- Students have some experience with mallet technique.

- Students have experience using body percussion (such as snapping, clapping, and patsching).

6. Finish the song, having students improvise measures 17 and 18 on instruments, ending on an F octave in measure 18. Also, perhaps have students improvise an echo on the repeated words in the B section using glockenspiels in F pentatonic or nonpitched percussion instruments.

7. Have the class perform the entire song several times, letting many students have an opportunity to improvise on the instruments.

Indicators of Success

- Students improvise measures in an appropriate rhythm using tones of the pentatonic scale.

Follow-up

- Do question-answer activities in 2/4, 4/4, and 6/8 meters. Have students perform both the questions and the answers. Over time, increase the complexity of the note and rhythm patterns.

STANDARD 3C

Improvising melodies, variations, and accompaniments: Students improvise simple rhythmic variations and simple melodic embellishments on familiar melodies.

Objective

■ Students will improvise rhythmic variations on and add melodic embellishments to parts of a familiar song in a stylistically correct manner.

Materials

■ "Dumplin's," in *Share the Music,* Grade 3 (New York: Macmillan/McGraw-Hill, 1995); *Music and You,* Grades 2 and 4 (New York: Macmillan/McGraw-Hill, 1991)

■ Flannel board with rhythm patterns notated (see figure on page 28) in movable quarter and eighth notes

Prior Knowledge and Experiences

■ Students can sing the correct pitches and rhythms of "Dumplin's."

Procedures

1. Have students sing the song "Dumplin's" with good breath support and tone. Without reference to the flannel board, ask students to echo the words "One of my dumplin's gone" in the various rhythms (A, B, and C).

2. Chant one of the rhythms on *ti's* and *ta's* without reference to the board. Then have students echo while you point to the notated rhythm. [*Note:* Students who have not learned to read rhythms may learn to read *ti's* and *ta's* quickly by association.] Chant the other rhythms, and have students echo as you point to the notes.

3. Challenge students to tell you which rhythm you are chanting. Chant rhythms A, B, and C in different orders.

4. Ask students to arrange quarter notes and eighth notes on the flannel board in different rhythmic configurations for the phrase "One of my dumplin's gone." Then let the class perform the phrase the way the students have arranged it, fitting the words and pitches to the new rhythms.

5. Tell students that you will sing the next phrase two times. Ask them to be ready to tell you whether the two ways you sing are alike or different. Model the phrase "Well, one of my dumplin's gone, Don't tell me so, One of my dumplin's gone" in pitches exactly as written. Then perform it scooping up to the pitch on "Well . . ."

6. When students determine that you sang differently the second time, ask one student to demonstrate how you sang the second phrase. Challenge students to experiment with scooping up to the pitch on one other word in the refrain. Let volunteers try one at the time. After several tries, they may find that this embellishment works best on "Well," "Don't," and the last "gone." [*Note:* This type of singing, when not overdone, is in keeping with one of the performance styles of songs from the West Indies.]

Indicators of Success

■ Students create new rhythm patterns from existing ones and embellish pitches intentionally as they sing.

(continued)

Follow-up

- Introduce the song "We Shall Overcome," in *The Music Connection,* Grades 4 and 8 (Parsippany, NJ: Silver Burdett Ginn, 1995); or *World of Music,* Grade 8 (Parsippany, NJ: Silver Burdett Ginn, 1991). Encourage students to experiment with embellishing pitches in the melody by scooping up or sliding down to them in Black gospel style.

Rhythm patterns for steps 1–3 (see Procedures).

STANDARD 3D

Improvising melodies, variations, and accompaniments: Students improvise short songs and instrumental pieces, using a variety of sound sources, including traditional sounds, nontraditional sounds available in the classroom, body sounds, and sounds produced by electronic means.

Objective

- Students will improvise short songs and instrumental accompaniments using classroom instruments, body percussion, and melodies they create themselves.

Materials

- Children's nursery rhymes appropriate for the students' age

- Short poems, such as "It's Baseball Time" (see step 1)

- Orff mallet instruments set in G pentatonic

- Nonpitched percussion instruments (such as Vibraslap, whip, triangle, or guiro)

Prior Knowledge and Experiences

- Students have experience playing Orff and other classroom instruments.

Procedures

1. Teach the poem "It's Baseball Time" by chanting and echoing one phrase at a time.

   > "It's baseball time; the crowd is here.
   >
   > 'Play ball!' the umpire cries.
   >
   > 'Strike one! Strike two!' and then a 'crack!'
   >
   > It's going, going, . . . GONE!"
   >
   > —Anonymous

2. When students can recite the poem independently, split the class into four groups and send each group to a mallet instrument set in G pentatonic. Break the poem into four phrases and assign a phrase to each group. Challenge each group to create a melody line for their phrase. Tell students that Group 1 must start the piece on G, and Group 4 must end the piece on G. Also, tell them they may use only G, A, B, D, and E (not F-sharp or C) in their melodies.

3. After five to eight minutes, ask a student from each group to teach the group's melody to the rest of the class by modeling. Have these students either sing alone or play the melody on the Orff instrument while singing. Be sure that each student who sings models correct posture, diction, and breath support. Tell class they should echo the model's singing.

4. When all the phrases have been taught and students have sung the song several times, add a chord or level bordun on the alto metallophone. Add other complimentary ostinatos on other pitched percussion instruments and layer them in as you wish, teaching all pitched percussion parts by body percussion first. Then have students transfer the body percussion to instruments.

5. Have students perform the piece with the ostinato accompaniment(s).

6. Give the groups five more minutes to choose one or two nonpitched percussion instruments to add to certain words in their phrases. Have the groups rehearse the piece with the nonpitched percussion instruments by chanting the text and adding the nonpitched percussion instruments where they choose.

(continued)

7. Have students perform the entire piece in ABA form as follows: chanting with nonpitched percussion, singing with pitched percussion, chanting with nonpitched percussion.

Indicators of Success

- Students improvise melodies and ostinato accompaniments for the selected poem.

- Students successfully perform the piece they have improvised, using a variety of classroom instruments to convey the text and the mood of the piece.

Follow-up

- Using other short nursery rhymes or poems, assign different phrases to each group, and repeat the procedures in this strategy.

- Have students experiment with creating short songs in C and F pentatonic.

STANDARD 4A

Composing and arranging music within specified guidelines: Students create and arrange music to accompany readings or dramatizations.

Objective

- Students will create a piece of music to accompany a chant or short poem.

Materials

- "Heaven Chant," in *Musical Games, Finger Plays, and Rhythmic Activities for Early Childhood,* by Marian Wirth, Verna Stassevitch, Rita Shotwell, and Patricia Stemmler (Old Tappan, NJ: Prentice-Hall, 1983)
- Pitched and nonpitched classroom percussion instruments
- Chalkboard or paper
- Audiocassette recorder, microphone, and blank tape; or video camera and videocassette recorder (optional)

Prior Knowledge and Experiences

- Students have experience with rhythmic speech and with playing simple rhythms on classroom percussion instruments.

Procedures

1. Teach students "Heaven Chant" in small segments by rote. Fully explore the different musical possibilities of each phrase. For example, vary and contrast tempo, dynamics, pitch, and meter.

2. Divide the class into four groups. Assign each group one of the four phrases of the chant, and have each group choose appropriate sounds, rhythms, and movements for its line, forming them into an ostinato.

3. Have each group perform its ostinato for the rest of the class.

4. Help students create an overall structure for the chant. Consider layers, repetition, and variations.

5. Have students perform the entire piece.

6. Notate the students' piece on the chalkboard or on paper. You might also make an audio recording or videotape to play for the class later and to have as a record of students' development.

Indicators of Success

- Students accurately complete the creation and organization of accompanying ostinatos for the chant.
- Students successfully perform their creation.

Follow-up

- Introduce more complex or extended compositional tasks, including having students complete more phrases independently, using more complex rhythms and exploring form and texture.

STANDARD 4B

Composing and arranging music within specified guidelines: Students create and arrange short songs and instrumental pieces within specified guidelines.

Objective

- Students will compose a piece in ABA (ternary) form.

Materials

- Pictures that illustrate contrast in the everyday environment
- Pitched and nonpitched classroom percussion instruments
- Chalkboard or paper

Prior Knowledge and Experiences

- Students have experience playing classroom percussion instruments and creating their own sound patterns.
- Students are familiar with the concepts of beat and rhythm.
- Students have experience using rhythmic and melodic notation.

Procedures

1. Discuss the concept of contrast, eliciting from the students examples of contrast in the world around them. Use verbal and visual illustrations.

2. Introduce the idea of creating contrast. Have students try to find other examples in the illustrations. Then transfer the concept to music with which the class is familiar.

3. Explain the concept of contrast and repetition in ternary form. Have the class suggest ways of contrasting A and B sections in music.

4. Have students, as a class or individually, experiment and finally decide on a four-measure A section and a contrasting four-measure B section using pitched and nonpitched percussion instruments.

5. Have students notate the sections that they have created on the chalkboard or on paper and arrange them in ABA form.

6. Have the class perform the piece and discuss the effectiveness of the repetition and contrast. Be prepared to modify the piece if appropriate.

Indicators of Success

- Students compose simple ternary-form compositions.

Follow-up

- To introduce rondo form, have students extend their compositions to a C section. Then have students develop simple accompaniments or compositions using the rondo form.

STANDARD 4C

Composing and arranging music within specified guidelines:
Students use a variety of sound sources when composing.

Objective

- Using a variety of "found" instruments, vocal sounds, and body percussion, students will create their own compositions, arrange them into a rondo, and perform the arrangement.

Materials

- Instruments created with found material at home or in the classroom (for each child, one pitched instrument or three nonpitched percussion instruments in three different sound categories; for example, bell-like, wooden, and metallic)
- Chalkboard or transparency
- Overhead projector, if transparency is used
- Audiocassette recorder, microphone, and blank tape

Prior Knowledge and Experiences

- Students have experimented with body percussion (snapping, clapping, patsching) and vocal sounds such as whistles, trills, and clicks.
- Students have completed a music-instrument-making project (see Materials).

Procedures

1. Have students look around the room and find new sound sources (such as an Orff mallet on the soundboard of a piano, a penny on a windowpane). Lead a brainstorming session, writing down student ideas on the chalkboard or a transparency.

2. Divide the class into small ensembles of four or five students. Ask each ensemble to create a short composition (about sixty seconds) using a variety of sounds from their new sound sources, homemade or class-made instruments, body percussion, and their repertoire of vocal sounds. Give time for experimentation, and circulate among the groups to assist in planning.

3. Have each ensemble perform its composition twice, asking the class to listen carefully so that they can make suggestions for improvement. Then discuss the listeners' ideas. Have each ensemble perform its composition a third time, incorporating some of the suggestions.

4. Tell students that they will be arranging their compositions in a rondo form; review the meaning of rondo. Designate one ensemble as the A section and the other ensembles as contrasting ones (B, C, D, etc.)

5. Have students perform their rondo. Record the final performance.

Indicators of Success

- Using found instruments, body percussion, and vocal sounds, students create, arrange, and perform a rondo.

Follow-up

- Have the entire class listen carefully to the recording of their rondo, and have them evaluate their performance.
- Using "The Shoemaker," a Danish folk song and dance from Marian Wirth, Verna Stassevitch, Rita Shotwell, and Patricia Stemmler's *Musical Games, Finger Plays, and Rhythmic Activities for Early Childhood* (Old Tappan, NJ: Prentice-Hall, 1983), have half the class sing the song and dance while the others create a rhythmic accompaniment using found sources.

STANDARD 5A

Reading and notating music: *Students read whole, half, dotted half, quarter, and eighth notes and rests in 2/4, 3/4, and 4/4 meter signatures.*

Objective

- Students will read half, quarter, and eighth notes and rests in 3/4 meter.

Materials

- "She's Like the Swallow," arr. Lori-Anne Doloff, unison, Level 1, in *We Will Sing* by Doreen Rao (New York: Boosey & Hawkes, 1993), Level 1, with audiocassette
- Audiocassette player

Prior Knowledge and Experiences

- Students can aurally identify 3/4 meter, perform it using body percussion, and state how many beats half notes and quarter notes receive in 3/4 meter.
- Students understand the terms *system, measure,* and *bar line.*
- Students have some experience using rhythm syllables.

Procedures

1. Using body percussion, review meter (2/4 = patsch-clap, 3/4 = patsch-clap-snap, 4/4 = patsch-clap-snap-clap). Perform these meters in body percussion with the students, and ask them to tell you how many beats are in each group. Choose a student to demonstrate each meter, and have class identify which meter each volunteer is performing. For each example, ask, "Which beat is the strongest?"

2. Have students listen to a recording of "She's Like the Swallow" and decide the meter by experimenting with body percussion beat patterns while they are listening. Ask a volunteer to identify the meter of this song.

3. Introduce children to the score by asking, "What system on which page begins with the word 'never'? What system on which page begins with the piano and the flute playing? In what measure do you begin to sing? How many measures are there in system two on the first page?" [*Note:* Even if all students are not familiar with score-reading terminology, they will catch on as you use words of the text and measure numbers printed on the page. Lead students to draw conclusions from familiar information that is printed on the page.]

4. While students follow their score, sing "She's Like the Swallow" on a neutral syllable, stopping at different times. Have students tell you where you stopped by citing page, system, measure, and word. Repeat this process from the beginning each time, until you have sung all the way through measure 20. Then have students sing the piece on a neutral syllable from the beginning through measure 20.

5. Have students read the text aloud and sing the song with text from the beginning to measure 20. Remind students to be attentive to proper breath support, posture, phrasing, and vowel formation.

6. Echo-chant on rhythmic syllables and clap measures 7–9 without allowing students to look at the score. Ask students to find which system, measures, and words on page 115 they chanted and clapped. Invite students to sing through measure 20, and instruct them to raise their hands when they sing a measure that contains a half note followed by a quarter note. Challenge students to discover other places in the music where this rhythm occurs. Chant and sing the pattern each time it appears. Use this process to find measures that contain only quarter notes and measures that contain quarter-note rests.

7. Conduct students as they stand and perform the piece through measure 20. Have them attend to proper posture, breath support, phrasing, and vowel formation.

Indicators of Success

- Students read and perform half notes, quarter notes, and eighth notes and rests in 3/4 meter.

Follow-up

- In the next class, perform the first twenty measures of this piece as a review, and then teach the rest of the piece using the process outlined in the Procedures.

- Have students sightsing other song fragments or short songs with half notes, quarter notes, and eighth notes and rests in 3/4 meter.

STANDARD 5B

Reading and notating music: Students use a system (that is, syllables, numbers, or letters) to read simple pitch notation in the treble clef in major keys.

Objective

- Students will read pitches in a major key in the treble clef using solfège syllables and hand signs.

Materials

- "Jubilate Deo" by Michael Praetorius, arr. Doreen Rao (New York: Boosey & Hawkes), OCTB6350, unison and round, Level 1—also in *We Will Sing* by Doreen Rao (New York: Boosey & Hawkes, 1993)

- Poster with staff lines, or chalkboard with lines, showing unison version of "Jubilate Deo" with measure numbers notated

Prior Knowledge and Experiences

- Students can demonstrate melodic direction aurally, visually, and vocally.

- Students can name the lines and spaces on a treble staff.

- Students understand the meaning of the term *measure*.

- Students can sing a solfège scale and demonstrate the Curwen hand signs.

Procedures

1. In the key of C major, model (by singing) simple pitch patterns with solfège and hand signs. Ask students to echo each pattern. Call attention to proper breath support and vowel formation.

2. Sing the last two measures of "Jubilate Deo," using solfège and hand signs, and have students echo these. As you are modeling this pattern, begin pointing to the corresponding measures on the board. Ask students to continue to echo as you model and point to the notes on the staff. Interchange solfège with letter names while modeling and pointing.

3. Sing the entire piece, and have students raise a hand each time *sol* occurs. Ask, "How many *sol*'s are there in this whole song? In what measure number does *sol* occur first?" Repeat this process for the syllable *do*.

4. Slowly model the entire piece, phrase by phrase, using solfège with hand signs, and invite students to echo. Repeat this step using pitch letter names.

5. While students follow their scores, sing the piece on a neutral syllable such as "loo," stopping on certain notes. Challenge students to tell you on what note you stopped by measure, word, syllable, and letter name.

6. Model the song with Latin words, having students echo. Challenge students to pay attention to correct pronunciation, phrasing, and breath support.

7. Have students perform the entire piece in unison two or three times in succession.

Indicators of Success

- Students accurately identify and perform *do* and *sol* using solfège and hand signs when they occur in an unfamiliar piece.

Follow-up

- Divide the class into two or three groups and perform "Jubilate Deo" in canon, using solfège, letter names, and words.

- Apply the same procedure to "A Child Is Born," arr. Doreen Rao, for unison voices in canon, Level 2, in *We Will Sing*.

STANDARD 5C

Reading and notating music: Students identify symbols and traditional terms referring to dynamics, tempo, and articulation and interpret them correctly when performing.

Objective

- Students will identify expressive symbols and markings and interpret them accurately when singing a choral piece.

Materials

- "The Path to the Moon" by Eric H. Thiman (New York: Boosey & Hawkes), OCTB6114, unison, Level 1—also in *We Will Sing* by Doreen Rao (New York: Boosey and Hawkes, 1993)

- Chalkboard, or chart, showing symbols for dynamics and expressive markings found in "The Path to the Moon"

Prior Knowledge and Experiences

- Students have learned the pitches, rhythms, and text of "The Path to the Moon."

- Students have been introduced to the terms *piano, forte, crescendo, decrescendo, system,* and *measure.*

Procedures

1. Review the terms *forte* and *piano* by patching a steady beat as students echo your example. Then, as you continue to patsch, look at or nod at the markings on the chalkboard and ask students to find the dynamic you are patching while they echo. Ask students for definitions of these markings, and have them answer in traditional musical terms. Have students perform their understanding by patching a steady beat while you point to *forte* and *piano* on the board. Repeat this process for *crescendo* and *decrescendo* and the other markings on the board.

2. Ask, "On what system do you find the first *piano* dynamic marking?" Have students perform the piece, raising their hands each time they sing at *piano* level. Repeat this process, assigning another signal for other dynamic markings found in the piece.

3. Tell students that you are going to sing the first phrase of the piece two ways. Encourage them to watch their music to determine which way the music indicates the phrase should be sung. [*Note:* Carry the phrase over at the slur in measure 6 the first time, and take a breath there the second time.] Call on a volunteer to identify the correct example of singing. Have the student tell why the first example was correct. Use words such as "phrase" and "slur" incidentally as you question, occasionally pointing to them in the students' music or drawing examples on the board if more help is needed.

4. Invite students to perform the first phrase with the slur while you indicate the slur in your conducting gesture. Challenge students to discover other places in the music where they might not want to breathe to break the phrase, for example, "sails" to "carry" (measure 11) and "sail" to "on" (measure 21). Ask them to draw in a slur at the places where you and they decide to carry the phrase through without taking a breath.

5. Repeat step 3 with the other expressive markings found in this piece (for example, *crescendo* and *decrescendo).*

6. Have students perform the entire piece, paying attention to proper breath support, diction, phrasing, and expressive markings.

(continued)

7. Ask students to suggest ways of performing this piece that they would like to remember for the next time they sing it. As they make suggestions, guide students to evaluate their own rehearsal. Help students list at least three things they did well and things they could improve.

Indicators of Success

- Students perform the piece with proper phrasing and dynamics.

Follow-up

- Distribute a familiar piece in which phrasing is optional. Break students into several groups and have them determine the places where they should not take a breath.

- Have each group perform its interpretation for the class and give reasons for its choices of slurs and breaths.

STANDARD 5D

Reading and notating music: Students use standard symbols to notate meter, rhythm, pitch, and dynamics in simple patterns presented by the teacher.

Objective

- Students will identify standard symbols for *forte* and *piano* and will notate dynamics in a simple song.

Materials

- "Zion's Children," in *The Music Connection,* Grade K (Parsippany, NJ: Silver Burdett Ginn, 1995); *Music and You,* Grade K (New York: Macmillan/McGraw-Hill, 1991); or *World of Music,* Grades K, 2, and 3 (Parsippany, NJ: Silver Burdett Ginn, 1991)

- Chart, or chalkboard, showing text and notes of "Zion's Children" with space for dynamics over and between the lines

- Chalkboard with the word *forte* written in red and the word *piano* written in blue

- Two *f*s made from red construction paper and two *p*s made from blue construction paper, all with tape on the back

- Two 3-by-5-inch cards for each student

Procedures

1. Clap a four-beat pattern (such as *ta, ta, ti-ti, ta*) and have students echo. Clap once *forte,* and then repeat the same passage *piano.* While students are echoing, point to the corresponding word that is written on the chalkboard. Ask students the meaning of *forte* and *piano* based on what they have just performed. Have them perform their understanding by patsching a steady beat at the correct dynamic level while you point to one of the corresponding words on the board.

2. Ask students to listen as you sing "Zion's Children" and to hold up one finger when you sing *piano* and five fingers when you sing *forte.* Sing the song, or parts of it, switching back and forth between the dynamic markings until students show an aural understanding of the difference between the dynamic levels and their markings.

3. Teach "Zion's Children" by having students echo one phrase at a time. Remind students of proper posture, breath support, phrasing, and vowel formation.

4. Ask students to sing their understanding of *forte* and *piano* by performing the piece with the dynamics that you will indicate by holding up the construction paper markings at different times.

5. Have four volunteers face the chart with "Zion's Children," each holding one of the construction paper *f*'s or *p*'s. Ask the volunteers to listen to the class perform the phrases and to place the appropriate markings at the beginning of the phrases. Conduct the class, having them sing at least two phrases loudly and two phrases softly. Ask the class to check their peers' markings to make sure they are correct. Give four other students an opportunity to place the markings as you and the class perform the piece changing the dynamics. Again, challenge the class to evaluate their peers' placement of the marks.

(continued)

Prior Knowledge and Experiences

- Students can keep a steady beat.

- Students can match pitches.

- Students can sing or play simple quarter-note and eighth-note rhythm patterns.

6. Divide students into two groups, and have each student draw an *f* on one 3-by-5-inch card and a *p* on the other. Let each group determine its own dynamic changes for "Zion's Children." After about a minute, invite one group to perform its version of the piece. Have the other students demonstrate their understanding of the dynamics that group chose by holding up an *f* when the group sings loudly and a *p* when the group sings softly. Give each group a turn at performing and evaluating.

7. Perform the piece as a class one final time using the dynamics that you or they determine. Be sure that your conducting gestures are consistent with the dynamics you are trying to communicate.

Indicators of Success

- Students perform "Zion's Children" with the dynamic changes that you conduct.

- Students demonstrate their understanding of *piano* and *forte* using traditional symbols to notate what they hear.

- Students respond to loud and soft singing by holding up the correct notation signs.

Follow-up

- Use this process to teach *crescendo* and *decrescendo*. First review *forte* and *piano*.

- Ask students to draw *crescendo* and *decrescendo* marks in response to the class's or your performance. Have them decide on which side of the *crescendo* or *decrescendo* mark to place the *forte* and *piano* after they have performed the *crescendo* and *decrescendo*.

STANDARD 6A

Listening to, analyzing, and describing music: Students
identify simple music forms when presented aurally.

Objective

■ Students will identify AABB
and AABA forms when pre-
sented aurally and when they
perform them.

Materials

■ "Sourwood Mountain," in
Share the Music, Grade 4
(New York: Macmillan/
McGraw-Hill, 1995); or
Music and You, Grade 5 (New
York: Macmillan/McGraw-
Hill, 1991)

■ "The Sally Gardens," arr.
Benjamin Britten (New York:
Boosey & Hawkes),
OCTB5448, unison, Level
1—also in *We Will Sing* by
Doreen Rao (New York:
Boosey & Hawkes, 1993),
with audiocassette

■ Two signs (for each student)
with "A" drawn on one and
"B" on the other

■ Audiocassette player

Prior Knowledge and Experiences

■ Students can distinguish
"same" or "different" rhythm
patterns when presented
aurally.

■ Students understand the terms
system and *measure.*

Procedures

1. Clap a rhythmic phrase and ask students to echo. Clap a second
phrase, and ask students to tell you whether it is the same as or
different from the first one. Designate the letter A for one phrase
and the letter B for the other. Clap the phrases in different orders,
and ask one student to hold up the correct sign (A or B) as you
clap each phrase and students echo.

2. Introduce and invite students to sing "Sourwood Mountain."
Then, as you sing the song on a neutral syllable, challenge students to raise their hands when they hear the end of a musical
thought. (After you have sung the notes for "Hey de-ing dang
did-dle al-ly day" on a neutral syllable, most students will raise
their hands.) Say, "Tell me if the next musical thought I sing is the
same or different." Then sing the next phrase. (Most will agree
that the two musical thoughts are the same.) Ask students whether
the two phrases should be called A and A or A and B. [*A and A.*]

3. Sing the song again, challenging students to raise their hands when
the musical thought changes or is different. Ask students to identify the word on which the musical thought changes. [*"My."*] Ask,
"Should we call this new thought A or B? Why?" Have students
sing the song as a group, and ask them to count the number of
times each A and B is heard in the first stanza. Have volunteers
tell you how they know that there are two As and two Bs. Have
one volunteer draw the letters on the board in the order of the
musical thoughts in "Sourwood Mountain." [*AABB.*]

4. Distribute the scores of "The Sally Gardens." Challenge students
to raise their hands when they hear the B section as they listen to
the recording. Ask, "How did you know it was the B section?"

5. Begin to familiarize students with the score by asking, "What system on page 99 begins with the word 'love'?" [*3*] "What system
begins with 'down'?" [*2*] "How many systems are there are on page
99?" [*3*] "How many systems are there on page 100?" [*4*] "How
many measures are there in system 2 on page 100?" [*3*] Have students listen to the recording again and ask them to put their finger
on the measure where the B section begins. Ask, "In what measure

(continued)

does the B section begin?" [*12*] "Does the A section return? On what words?" [*But I, being young and foolish, . . .*] Challenge students to draw the order of As and Bs in the first stanza of this piece. [*AABA.*]

6. Teach "The Sally Gardens" by singing from the beginning on a neutral syllable. Ask students to follow the notes with their fingers as you sing from the beginning, stopping at different times. Ask them to identify where you stopped by telling you the specific page, system, measure, and word. Repeat this process, starting at the beginning each time, until you reach the end of the A section. Ask students to sing the A section on a neutral syllable. Chant the text in short, rhythmic phrases, and have students echo. Sing the A section in short, rhythmic phrases as students echo. Invite students to sing the piece from the beginning, and then repeat the process for the B section. Conduct the entire piece through as the students sing.

7. After students have sung the whole first stanza, ask them if this song has the same form as "Sourwood Mountain." Ask, "What do the forms of the songs have in common? How are the forms different?" [*Both have A and B sections; in "The Sally Gardens," the A section comes back after B.*]

Indicators of Success

■ Students identify AABB and AABA form when they hear a song in this form.

Follow-up

■ Use this procedure to teach forms other than two-part or rounded binary. Rondo form can be taught from the song "Ching-a-Ring Chaw," arr. Aaron Copland (New York: Boosey & Hawkes), OCTB6609, unison, Level 2—also in *We Will Sing* by Doreen Rao (New York: Boosey & Hawkes, 1993). [*Note:* "Ching-a, ring-a, ring ching ching" is the rondo theme.]

STANDARD 6B

Listening to, analyzing, and describing music: Students demonstrate perceptual skills by moving, by answering questions about, and by describing aural examples of music of various styles representing diverse cultures.

Objective

- Students will perform with appropriate movement and describe what they hear in a song from South Africa and in chants of the Inuit people of Alaska.

Materials

- "Siyahamba," arr. Doreen Rao (New York: Boosey & Hawkes), OCTB6656, three-part, Level 2

- Recording of "Siyahamba," from *Glen Ellyn Children's Chorus 25th Anniversary Celebration* (available from Glen Ellyn Children's Chorus, 586 Duane St., Suite 102, Glen Ellyn, IL 60137), audio-cassette

- Recording of "Nukapi-anguaq," from *Amabile Youth Singers* (93 Langarth Street W., London, ON, Canada, N6J1P5), IBS 1001, compact disc

- Two chants from "Nukapi-anguaq" (Inuit chants), arr. Stephen Hatfield (New York: Boosey & Hawkes), OCTB6700, four-part (mostly unison/two-part), Level 2

- Audio-playback equipment

- Conga drum

Procedures

1. As students listen to the recording of "Siyahamba," challenge them to raise their hands when they hear the melody being hummed. Have students listen again and indicate when they hear the melody sung in Zulu. Ask, "In what other language did you hear the melody?" [*English.*]

2. Teach the soprano line of "Siyahamba" by rote in Zulu.

3. Ask students to sing the text in English and move as the text suggests: On the words "We are marching in the light of God," have students lean over and march in place with both hands and feet, as in slow motion, and keep a steady beat; on the word "light," have them stand straight and raise their hands above their heads with fingers spread and hands shaking.

4. Improvise a simple rhythm pattern accompaniment on the conga drum as students sing in Zulu first, swaying from side to side on the beat. Have students sing the second stanza in English with the suggested movement. Then have them sing the final stanza in Zulu.

5. Ask students to listen to the recording of "Nukapianguaq" and raise their hands when they think they hear the "goose chant." Have students describe characteristics of this chant that sound different from most children's choir music. [*Nasal quality.*]

6. Teach students the first two chants from "Nukapianguaq." Have students describe the sounds of these chants of the Inuit people of Alaska. [*Whispered and grunting sound in the first chant; nasal, plaintive sound in the second chant.*]

Indicators of Success

- Students describe an example of music of South Africa and of Inuit chants.

- Students move appropriately to the music that they sing and hear.

(continued)

Prior Knowledge and Experiences

- Students have experience singing simple unison songs a cappella.

Follow-up

- Have students perform "Siyahamba" with movement for another class or for a school program.

- Have students listen to "Friendship Song," from *Glen Ellyn Children's Chorus 25th Anniversary Celebration,* and raise their hands when they hear the melody being sung in English. Then teach the song by rote from the score—"Friendship Song," arr. Doreen Rao (New York: Boosey & Hawkes, 1993), OCTB6616, unison and round, Level 1—first in Czech, then in English. Have them perform this piece in English as a two-part canon. Later, extend it to a three- or four-part canon.

STANDARD 6C

Listening to, analyzing, and describing music: Students use appropriate terminology in explaining music, music notation, music instruments and voices, and music performances.

Objective

- Students will use musical or technical terms when discussing a musical score or a musical performance.

Materials

- "The Raggle Taggle Gypsies," arr. Robert Hugh (New York: Boosey & Hawkes), OCTB6747, two-part, Level 2

Prior Knowledge and Experiences

- Students have classroom choral experience and are familiar with score-reading terms such as *score, system, measure, bar line, meter signature, treble clef, bass clef,* and *key signature.*

- Students have a performing knowledge of dynamics.

Procedures

1. Give students the octavo for "The Raggle Taggle Gypsies" and introduce them to the written score by asking, "What system begins with the word 'gypsies'?" "What measure number is at the beginning of system 3?" "In what measure do the voices enter?" "What is the meter signature of system 3, measure 3?" [*Note:* There are mixed meters in this piece.] "What other measures in this piece have this same meter signature?"

2. After students have given their answers, begin introducing the melody by singing from the beginning on the neutral syllable "loo" as students follow the melody in their scores. Stop from time to time and ask students to tell you where you stopped by having them cite page, system, measure, and word. Be sure you start at the beginning each time you sing the melody.

3. After you have sung the first page through measure 16, return to the double bar and stop after a measure or two. Ask students to identify where you are and to explain why you returned to the beginning of the second system. [*There is a repeat mark.*] Ask them how many times you will repeat systems 2–4. Then challenge students to tell you where singers should go in the music after singing systems 2–4 the third time. Ask them to identify other double bars in the piece.

4. Teach the remainder of the song using the same process.

5. Ask, "How many voice parts are there on the third system of page 5?" Ask a volunteer to tell you what the text means and who might have sung this song. Demonstrate the dynamic contrasts, and have students describe them using musical terms after they hear you perform them. Ask them to find similar dynamics in the rest of the piece.

6. Have students perform the entire piece. Direct students' attention to proper posture, breath support, diction, tone quality, and dynamics.

7. Stimulate class discussion about the performance of the piece. Use musical terminology in your questions and encourage students to respond with correct terminology. Ask students to suggest things about the performance that went well and things that need improvement.

(continued)

Indicators of Success

- Students use musical terms when identifying places in the score or when talking about their performance.

Follow-up

- Use a similar procedure to teach students to read the score of "Oliver Cromwell," arr. Benjamin Britten (New York: Boosey & Hawkes), OCTB5893, unison, Level 1—also in *We Will Sing* by Doreen Rao (New York: Boosey & Hawkes, 1993).

STANDARD 6D

Listening to, analyzing, and describing music: Students identify the sounds of a variety of instruments, including many orchestra and band instruments, and instruments from various cultures, as well as children's voices and male and female adult voices.

Objective

- Students will identify instruments, a child's voice, and male and female adult voices when they are presented aurally.

Materials

- Recording of *Baroque Duet—Kathleen Battle and Wynton Marsalis*, SONY SK 46672

- Recording of *Requiem*, op. 48, by Gabriel Fauré, TELARC 80135

- Recording of Leonard Bernstein's *Chichester Psalms*, CBS Records MK 44710

- Choral score of Leonard Bernstein's *Chichester Psalms* (New York: Boosey & Hawkes), LCB214

- Recorded examples of harpsichord music and piano music

- Pictures of harpsichord and harp

- Audio-playback equipment

Prior Knowledge and Experiences

- Students have experience singing unison songs.

- Students have experience identifying aurally instruments such as piano, trumpet, and violin.

Procedures

1. Play the recording of "Let the Bright Seraphim," by George Frideric Handel, track 1 from *Baroque Duet*. Challenge students to listen for the trumpet and raise their hands or stand up when they hear it. Ask, "Is a man or a woman singing on this recording?"

2. While showing a picture of a harpsichord, play a recorded example of harpsichord music. Ask students whether this instrument looks like a piano and ask, "How is it the same? How is it different? Does it sound the same as a piano?" Continue to ask questions and guide the discussion until students understand that strings on a harpsichord are plucked, while piano strings are struck with felt hammers. Play examples of both instruments, challenging students to distinguish between the two.

3. Play "Su le sponde del Tebro," first movement, by Alessandro Scarlatti, track 6 from *Baroque Duet,* and challenge students to raise their hands or stand each time they hear the harpsichord.

4. Invite students to listen to "Libera me," from the Fauré *Requiem.* Challenge them to let you know by raising hands, holding up fingers, standing, or in another way that you determine, when the male soloist sings, and again when the whole choir enters. Ask, "Is the choir on the recording a children's choir or an adult choir? Is the soloist a child or a man?" On the "Sanctus" of the *Requiem,* have students identify the solo violin and places where men sing alone and women sing alone.

5. Play the first part of track 8, "Psalm 23," from *Chichester Psalms,* and ask students to identify the type of voice that is singing. [*Boy soprano.*] Ask, "What instrument is accompanying the soloist?" Have a picture of a harp, and be prepared to ask students how they think the harp is played. Using a choral score of *Chichester Psalms,* teach students the first solo of the boy soprano part by rote. Ask them to sing along with the recording.

Indicators of Success

- Students identify correctly the sounds of female and male adult voices, child's voice, trumpet, violin, harpsichord, and harp.

(continued)

Follow-up

- Have students listen to other recordings of choral or vocal music and instruments, especially those that contain children's voices; for example, the fifth movement from *St. Nicholas,* op. 42, by Benjamin Britten, Hyperion Records CDA66333; or *An Amabile Festival,* featuring the Amabile Youth Singers (93 Langarth Street W., London, ON, Canada N6J1P5), IBS 1005, compact disc.

STANDARD 6E

Listening to, analyzing, and describing music: Students respond through purposeful movement to selected prominent music characteristics or to specific music events while listening to music.

Objective

■ Students will perform movements suggested by a song and respond to a specific music event while listening to the song.

Materials

■ "Hello Song," from *Share the Music,* Grade K (New York: Macmillan/McGraw-Hill, 1995); or *Music and You,* Grade K (New York: Macmillan/McGraw-Hill, 1991)

Prior Knowledge and Experiences

■ Students have experience singing simple a cappella songs in unison.

Procedures

1. Teach "Hello Song" by echo-singing through measure 8. Listen for correct pitch-matching. Use your hand to indicate pitch levels.

2. Sing measures 9–12 for students, cuing them to follow the directions in the text of the song. Repeat (changing colors or words) measures 9–12 until students can anticipate the word "up." Challenge them to be ready to stand exactly on that word. Sing the part several times, changing the words to include all the students. Intermittently, go back to the beginning, and direct all students to sing with you on measures 1–8.

3. Work on pitches that are not secure in measures 1–8. Sing through measures 9–12, choosing new words each time. See how many students can anticipate the exact time of "up" each time and stand accordingly.

4. Teach measures 13–16 by echo and imitation. Model patsching, stamping, and nodding on the beat (four beats per measure). Repeat this part several times, encouraging students to sing and do the movement on the beat. If their movement is not on the beat, try a different movement (on the first and third stanzas) on beats two and four; for example, patsch-clap-patsch-clap, and nod-clap-nod-clap.

Indicators of Success

■ Students anticipate the word "up" in the song and stand on time.

■ Students perform the appropriate movements with the beat while singing the song.

■ Students demonstrate an increasing ability to keep a steady beat and sing the song on the correct pitches.

Follow-up

■ Invite students to sing "Hello Song" and do the movements at the beginning of many music classes.

■ As students improve in their ability to keep a steady beat, have them transfer the body percussion rhythms they have learned to nonpitched percussion instruments.

STANDARD 7A

Evaluating music and music performances: Students devise criteria for evaluating performances and compositions.

Objective

- Students will create a recorded model of correct Latin vowel diction, identify criteria that make it a good model, and compare their singing of newly learned Latin phrases to the model and correct their diction.

Materials

- "In Dulci Jubilo," by Johann Sebastian Bach, arr. Doreen Rao, in *We Will Sing* by Doreen Rao (New York: Boosey & Hawkes, 1993), unison, Level 1

- Chart of International Phonetic Alphabet Symbols for certain vowels.

  [i] = ee as in feet

  [ε] = eh as in bed

  [α] = ah as in father

  [o] = o as in obey (not oh + ooh; no diphthong)

  [u] = ooh as in food

- Chart or chalkboard showing the following text notated in IPA symbols with consonants:

  [i]n d[u]l-ch[i] y[u]-b[i]-l[o]

  [i]n pr[ε]-s[ε]-p[i]-[o]

- Audiocassette recorder, microphone, and blank tape

Procedures

1. Conduct students through warm-ups on neutral syllables constructed from the IPA vowel sounds on the chart; for example, [u] [i], [u] [i]; [i] [ε], [i] [ε]; [i] [α], [i] [α]; [i]-[ε]-[α]-[o]-[u] on any combination of tones. Have students vocalize up and down the scale.

[i]   [ε]   [α]   [o]   [i] [ε] [α][o] [u]   [i]   [ε]   [α]

2. Echo-chant the phrase "In dulci jubilo" ([i]n d[u]l-ch[i] y[u]-b[i]-l[o]). Then echo-sing the phrase, paying particular attention to pure Latin vowel sounds. Ask students to sing the phrase several times, and correct any incorrect vowel sounds. Call particular attention to the word "in," which should be [i]n rather than "ih-n." Have students round the lips rather than spreading them too much on [i]. Point to the notation of the text in IPA as they sing. Repeat this step for the phrase "in praesepio ([i]n pr[ε]-s[ε]-p[i]-[o]).

3. When students' singing of the two phrases just learned is an accurate model of pitch and diction, record the students immediately. Play the tape for students and ask them to identify what makes their singing on the recording an accurate model.

4. Sing on the neutral syllable "la" the notes of the phrases "Matris in gremio" and "Alpha es et O." Invite students to echo.

5. Challenge students to try to pronounce the Latin text. Let them chant it on their own once. Remind students to listen to each other and to match pitch. Then ask them to sing the Latin text as you record their performance.

Prior Knowledge and Experiences

- As a group, students can sing pitches and rhythms of "In Dulci Jubilo" on a neutral syllable.

- Students can find specific measures in a score.

6. Play the model tape of the first two examples again. Then play the last two examples. Have students compare the diction on the two tapes. Ask them to decide whether [i] in "matris" sounds like [i] in "dulci" and "jubilo"; whether [ɛ] in "es" and "et" sounds like [ɛ] in "praesepio"; whether [o] in "gremio" sounds like [o] in "jubilo."

7. Ask students to perform the whole song, paying attention to correct diction, especially in the Latin phrases. If you choose, record them again. Help students decide whether their diction in the last two Latin phrases is as correct as in the first two Latin phrases.

Indicators of Success

- Students sing a correct model of vowel sounds according to the International Phonetic Alphabet.

- Students distinguish between correct and incorrect vowel sounds and adjust their vowels accordingly.

Follow-up

- As students become more familiar with the International Phonetic Alphabet, have them draw correct sound symbols over text syllables in their music that are difficult to pronounce correctly; for example, "[ɑ]" over the word "night" will help them to prolong the initial vowel sound and prevent them from going to the diphthong too soon.

STANDARD 7B

Evaluating music and music performances: Students explain, using appropriate terminology, their personal preferences for specific musical works and styles.

Objective

- Students will perform a song in two different styles, choosing a style they prefer and stating a reason for their preference using appropriate musical terms.

Materials

- Chart, or chalkboard, showing the following rhythm pattern that is basic to swing eighths:

Prior Knowledge and Experiences

- Students can sing a simple, two-part a cappella song.

Procedures

1. Have students echo-chant the rhythm illustrated on the chart two times without your calling attention to the chart. Give each eighth note equal emphasis. Have students echo-chant the rhythm two more times while you point to the notation.

2. Echo-chant the eighth notes in swing style as follows:

After students have chanted the pattern in the new style, point to the chart as they chant, touching the eighth notes in the chart as if they were notated in swing style. Ask students to listen as you sing the refrain of "Jingle Bells" in both rhythms and to be ready to tell you which version is in swing style. [*Note:* This strategy is based on the assumption that many children can learn terminology as it is spoken and performed in context. Explaining and defining should be used to clarify concepts after children have had a chance to associate and discover.] After you sing the refrain both ways, call on a volunteer to identify the version that was in swing rhythm and the one that was in "strict" rhythm. (Most will correctly identify the swing version.)

3. Ask students to count aloud "1-2-3-4" in a slow tempo as you sing the refrain of "Jingle Bells" in swing rhythm. Snap on 2 and 4 and cue them to join you. Ask, "On what beats am I snapping?"

4. Ask students to sing through the refrain of "Jingle Bells" in straight rhythm once and in swing rhythm once. On the swing version, add a snap on beats 2 and 4. Ask, "On what beats do we snap when we sing in jazz style?"

5. Now ask students to sing the refrain of "Jingle Bells" in a swing rhythm using scat syllables as follows:

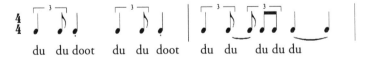

6. Sing the whole refrain on words in swing rhythm, and teach your version to the students.

7. Ask students to choose one of the following statements to complete. Tell them that they must use one of the musical terms that was used to talk about the music ("swing," "jazz," or "scat").

> I like to sing "Jingle Bells" in _____ style. The eighth notes are sung in a _____ rhythm. I like to sing in _____ syllables.

or

> I like to sing "Jingle Bells" the old way. I feel more comfortable singing the eighth notes even rather than in _____ style. I would rather sing real words than _____ syllables.

Indicators of Success

- Using correct terminology, students describe a musical style that they like after performing a song in two different styles.

Follow-up

- Introduce "Jingle Bell Swing," arr. David Elliott, two-part, Level 2, in *We Will Sing* by Doreen Rao (New York: Boosey & Hawkes, 1993). Depending on children's ability, have them sing or listen to the song.

STANDARD 8A

Understanding relationships between music, the other arts, and disciplines outside the arts: Students identify similarities and differences in the meanings of common terms used in the various arts.

Objective

- Students will identify strophic, binary, and ternary forms in songs, architectural structures, and visual art, and relate them to one another through response, discussion, and creation of artworks.

Materials

- Songs or compositions that model simple musical forms such as strophic (AA), binary (AB), and ternary (ABA)

- Photographs or drawings of famous architectural structures (see step 2)

- Photographs or drawings of local architectural structures that demonstrate these simple forms

- Books of art that have many examples of paintings or drawings

- Drawing or painting materials (such as pencils, chalk, charcoal, or paints)

Prior Knowledge and Experiences

- Students have experience recognizing aural and visual patterns.

Procedures

1. Teach or review songs that demonstrate simple musical forms. Explain how music has similar and contrasting melodies and/or sections that form an overall pattern. Be sure that names for these patterns (strophic, AA; binary, AB; and ternary, ABA) emerge in discussion of the musical forms.

2. Show famous structures such as the Cathedral of Notre Dame in Paris (ternary), the Capitol building in Washington D.C. (ternary), the Opera House in Sydney, Australia (strophic), the United Nations Building in New York City (binary), the Parthenon in Athens (strophic). Ask students to identify which songs from their repertoire might have a similar form.

3. Show students pictures of local, familiar buildings for comparison of architectural form with musical form. Challenge students to pair musical forms with corresponding architectural forms.

4. Show photographs or prints of works of art that demonstrate the simple forms just taught. Ask students to identify songs previously learned that have similar forms.

5. Have students do one of the following: (1) Draw a local building that demonstrates one of the various forms taught, identify the form of the building, and match it with a known song or piece of music of the same form; (2) Create a work of art that uses one of the musical forms in its design, and pair the artwork with a known song of the same form.

Indicators of Success

- Students identify strophic, binary, and ternary forms in songs, architectural structures, and visual art.

- Students demonstrate their understanding of the relation of these forms to one another through response, discussion, and creation of artworks.

Follow-up

- Go outside with the students, look at the structure of the school building, and have students compare its structural form to one of the previously learned songs that has a similar form.

- As a homework assignment, have students find examples of each of the three musical forms in the physical world outside the school. (A truck and a trailer, for example, could represent AB form.)

STANDARD 8B

Understanding relationships between music, the other arts, and disciplines outside the arts:
Students identify ways in which the principles and subject matter of other disciplines taught in the school are interrelated with those of music.

Objective

- Students will identify poems of several English poets whose texts have been set to music and will describe how the music illustrates the mood or feeling of the poem.

Materials

- "Orpheus with His Lute" by Ralph Vaughan Williams (New York: Oxford University Press), OCS52, unison, Level 1

- "When Cats Run Home" by Eric H. Thiman (New York: Boosey and Hawkes), OCTB5570, two-part canon, Level 1

- "The Ferryman" by Dorothy Parke (Toronto: Gordon V. Thompson Music), G-143, unison, Level 1

Prior Knowledge and Experiences

- Students can sing in unison and in two-part canon.

- Students have been studying poetry in the language classroom.

Procedures

1. Have students read with you the poem "Orpheus with His Lute" from the octavo. As a result of questioning and discussions, have students define any less-known terms, such as *lute*. Have a student tell the story of the character Orpheus in Greek mythology: Orpheus was a poet-musician with magical musical powers who tried to lead his wife Eurydice back from the Underworld. He did not succeed because he looked back when instructed not to do so. Challenge students to find the composer's name on the page.

2. Have another student find the author of the text (whose name appears in the top left-hand corner of the octavo): William Shakespeare, 1564–1616; English poet who used the Greek mythological story and set it in poetic form.

3. Have students sing through the selection or listen to you perform the piece. Discuss how the music enhances the text through legato phrasing, through-composed setting, varying phrase lengths, and dynamics. Question and discuss how the mood of the poem affects the melody and tempo of music and how the energy or motion of the text syllables affect the rhythm of the music.

4. Provide similar brief overviews of poetry and authorship for "When Cats Run Home" by Eric Thiman, with text by Alfred Lord Tennyson, 1809–1892, English poet; and "The Ferryman" by Dorothy Parke, which uses a poem by Christina Rossetti, 1830–1894, English poet.

5. Have students study the scores of both works and tell why Thiman uses staccato articulation to portray the text and why Parke uses a rondo or repeated form to depict the dialogue between characters in the poem.

6. Lead a discussion of some of the techniques used to match text to music and music to text. Review the names of authors and composers.

7. Have students sing "Orpheus and His Lute" as an ensemble.

Indicators of Success

- Students identify three English poets and discuss ways the composers chose to set the poetry to music.

Follow-up

- Have students learn to sing "Orpheus with His Lute," "When Cats Run Home," and "The Ferryman" and perform them in a concert.

- Have students select poems, set them to music, and perform them for the class.

STANDARD 9A

Understanding music in relation to history and culture: Students identify by genre or style aural examples of music from various historical periods and cultures.

Objective

- Students will place their choral repertoire into periods or cultures and will discuss pertinent stylistic characteristics, avoiding stereotypical generalizations and oversimplifications.

Materials

- Choral music in the group's current repertoire
- Large pieces of paper with the titles of the pieces in the chorus's current repertoire, one sheet per piece (allowing space for additional words)

Prior Knowledge and Experiences

- Students have been introduced to various composers, lyricists, and folk traditions (such as country, bluegrass, gospel, and pop).

Procedures

1. Ask a variety of questions that stimulate a class discussion that will help students conclude that (a) the music they are rehearsing comes from many sources and is sung by children in many places; (b) it is good to know where a song comes from so that it can be performed in the appropriate style; and (c) many people in the audience will not know anything about some of the songs.

2. State the purpose of the activity; for example, "At our spring concert, members of the choir will introduce the songs. Perhaps you would like to do this. Perhaps you would like to help someone else do it. During this period, we will look at all our songs and try to decide what we should tell the audience that would help them to enjoy the music more."

3. Choose a piece and ask questions to stimulate students' thinking. For example, "Look at [*title of piece*]. Who wrote the music? The words? Could these people be alive today? When did they live? Can you guess where they might have lived? What gives you a clue about the composer's nationality? Does the song tell you anything about the composer or lyricist? What do you think is the most interesting part of this song? Why? What else? Of all the things we have talked about, what should we tell the audience?" As students review their responses, write down key words on the sheet with this song title.

4. Have students sing through several of the songs. Engage the class in discussion about how the songs sound and how the sounds are related to the style or cultural context of the song.

5. Divide the class into groups. Assign a song to each, giving each group the appropriate sheet, and encourage students to write key words or phrases that describe the song.

6. Ask students in each group to present their observations to the class. Give hints about cultural or stylistic elements of which they may be unaware but that merit research. Assign topics about style and culture for study, and set a time for the groups to report. In the assignment, have students put the key words and something from their research into sentences. As you listen to their reports, be alert for stereotypical language and generalizations as well as oversimplifications. Guide students to a sensible but accurate portrayal of the stylistic and cultural context of the music in their repertoire.

7. Invite students to present to you a written introduction for each piece.

Indicators of Success

- Students transfer contextual knowledge from pieces they know, responding with increasing accuracy to pertinent questions about genre, style, and cultural context when new music is introduced.

- Students perform music with increasing authenticity of style.

- Students recognize a number of different styles in new music they hear.

Follow-up

- Have students study and perform choral music in a variety of styles from various cultures.

- Include music in two or more languages on a concert, and assign students to provide accurate modern translations for the audience.

STANDARD 9B

Understanding music in relation to history and culture: Students describe in simple terms how elements of music are used in music examples from various cultures of the world.

Objective

- Students will use the elements of music to provide a structure for comparing, describing, and analyzing music of different cultures.

Materials

- Contrasting songs or listening selections from two or three different cultures that are represented in the group's current repertoire
- Copy (for each student) of Music Analysis Guide (see figure and step 3), scaled-down to include one to three elements and no more than two musical works, as appropriate for students' age
- Transparency of Music Analysis Guide
- Overhead projector

Prior Knowledge and Experiences

- Students have studied the basic elements of music, such as melody, rhythm, harmony, and form.
- Students have experience singing, playing, and moving to songs from other cultures.

Procedures

1. Have students sing a song from their repertoire. Ask questions that help students paraphrase and interpret the text. If the song is about farmers in Brazil, for example, you might ask, "What do these words tell us about farmers in Brazil? Why would farmers in Brazil sing this song?"

2. Ask questions that help students relate this song to songs of their own culture; for example, "Can you think of an American (or another culture's) song that (farmers in [*country name*]) might sing after a long day? How are (farmers in Brazil) and (farmers in [*country name*]) alike? How are they different? How is their music the same or different?"

3. Show the transparency of the Music Analysis Guide, listing the elements of music in vocabulary known to the students in an order that will elicit responses from them. Ask questions that will help students understand how to use it.

4. Lead students through one or more activities that help them focus on the elements of music, such as the following approaches to focusing on rhythm and melody: Echo-chant with the students a part of the text that is especially characteristic of the piece's style (such as syncopation). Have students sing parts or all of the song again, giving them the chance to listen specifically for rhythm. Say, "As we sing the song again, listen especially to the rhythm. Is it mostly even or uneven? After we sing, raise your hand if you think you know." Select a part of the melody that is especially characteristic. Ask students to tell you after singing it whether the melody went mostly up or down, and whether it did so in steps or skips.

5. Distribute copies of the Music Analysis Guide. Have students use it to compare songs of two or more cultures and to compare one or more elements of music among the pieces.

Indicators of Success

- Students give appropriate responses to questions about elements of music in the selected song.
- Students analyze, compare, and contrast two or more songs from different cultures.

Follow-up

- In subsequent choral rehearsals, have students demonstrate their understanding by making comparisons of music of various cultures regularly.

- Refer often to the elements of music as they appeared in other songs, and have students compare them to those of the song they are currently singing.

Music Analysis Guide

Elements of Music	Music of _____ Piece #1	Music of _____ Piece #2	Music of _____ Piece #3
Dynamics (loud, soft, gradual, sudden)			
Tempo (fast, slow, moderate)			
Rhythm (even, uneven)			
Melody (up, down, same, skips, steps)			
Harmony (2-, 3-, or 4-part)			
Form (same, different)			

STANDARD 9C

Understanding music in relation to history and culture: Students identify various uses of music in their daily experiences and describe characteristics that make certain music suitable for each use.

Objective

- Students will select music for performance in a program called "Music in Our Lives," justifying and describing their choices.

Materials

- Chalkboard or chart
- Representative octavos from students' choral repertoire

Prior Knowledge and Experiences

- Students have sung a variety of songs that focus on music in daily life, including songs on topics such as animals, work, patriotism, camp, worship, moods, love, neighbors, or political, environmental, or cultural issues.

Procedures

1. Ask questions that cause students to think about music in their lives, such as, "What music have you heard today? What were you doing when you heard it? Were you happy that you heard it, or did it annoy you? Why was the music being played? How would [*name an event*] have been different if you had had no music? When do you like to hear or listen to music? When do you not like to hear or listen to music? Why do producers use music in television shows and movies?"

2. As students are responding, extract words that help them to see the many functions of music in their own lives and the lives of their communities. Write these key words on the chalkboard. Responses might include the following: as a cue, to announce or gain attention, to mobilize, to entertain, for recreation, to advertise, to express an emotion, to express an opinion, to carry a message, for dance, for contemplation, to tell a story, to create a mood.

3. Have several examples of familiar choral music ready that students can relate to their lives. Help students connect their own daily experiences with some of the songs in the choral repertoire. For example, ask, "Can you think of a song that we have sung that tells a story? That expresses a feeling or mood? That is good for dancing?"

4 Divide students into small groups to select two or three songs that seem to serve a similar function. Let students suggest common themes that tie the songs together for possible use as headers for a concert program. Ask, "What is it about the songs that causes you to feel that they have a common theme? The texts? The subjects? The moods? The period of time in which they were written?" If students choose songs with contrasting functions, ask them what makes the songs appropriate for different situations. "Are the differences apparent mainly from the texts? The tempos? The styles? The themes?" For the songs or groups of songs, challenge students to prepare brief introductions that could be read to parents and other students who attend the performance.

Indicators of Success

- Students give thoughtful answers that identify characteristics in music that relate it to their lives.

- Students select songs and offer ideas for introductions that connect the music to daily experiences.

Follow-up

- Ask students to bring to class examples of experiences that caused them to think about a choral piece that they have sung, or have them tell of an incident when one of their songs reminded them of a particular experience. Challenge students to try to decide why the particular song had meaning for them in the specific experience.

STANDARD 9D

__Understanding music in relation to history and culture:__ Students identify and describe roles of musicians in various music settings and cultures.

Objective

- Students will discuss and analyze the roles of musicians (composers, performers, musician teachers) in their own lives, in the community, and in a culture or period they are studying in social studies.

Materials

- Large sheet of paper for wall charts
- Crayon or felt-tip pen

Prior Knowledge and Experiences

- Students can describe what composers and other musicians do.
- Many of the students sing in a school or community choir or an ensemble in a place of worship.
- Many students attend performances.

Procedures

1. Initiate the discussion of musicians by asking, "Do you know someone who performs music? Why do you think she plays (sings)? How did he learn?" Extend the discussion to include other performers that students know personally. Ask, "What other kinds of performers are there?"

2. Discuss the students' role as performers by asking, "Are you a performer? Who has heard you sing in the chorus? How did the chorus's music make the audience feel?"

3. Turn the students' attention to the role of composers. "Where do the performers get their music to play? Who writes it? Can you buy it? What does a composer do? Who writes the words? Where do composers get their ideas? Have you ever made up a song? Where did you get your idea for the song? What would happen if no one composed music?"

4. Focus on the role of the music teacher. "Why does our school have a music teacher? What do I do?" Extend the discussion to include other music teachers.

5. Help students to realize the importance of the variety of musicians' roles by suggesting a way of life without musicians. Ask, "If everyone stopped composing music, singing, and playing instruments, what would happen?" The importance of every musician's role should become apparent to the students as they contemplate and discuss the absence of performers, composers, and music teachers from their lives.

6. Bring the focus on musicians to a more personal level. For example, say to students, "Think of a musician that you would like to talk to in person or on the telephone. Write down three questions you would like to ask that person." Have each student name a musician in the community to interview. Write the musician's name on the wall chart. Try to help students think of as many different names as possible. Guide their attempts to think of questions to ask. Make the interview an assignment, and set a time for students to report their findings to the class.

7. Relate the discussion on musicians to a unit they are studying in social studies (for example, Black History Month). Think of gospel singers, players, or choir directors the students might want to interview. Extend the discussion to holidays or customs observed by different cultural or religious groups in the community (for example, Hispanic, Asian, Scandinavian, and Greek communities). Challenge students to interview members of these community groups who perform the music of their cultures.

Indicators of Success

- Students give appropriate answers, complete the assigned tasks, and share and listen to information about the roles of musicians in their own and other cultures.

- Students speak in an informed manner about various kinds of musicians in their community.

Follow-up

- Have students list all the music and music-related careers that they can identify in their community.

- Invite people who represent a variety of music careers (such as a music therapist, a musician from a place of worship, or a music merchant) to the class for a discussion of their work.

STANDARD 9E

Understanding music in relation to history and culture: Students demonstrate audience behavior appropriate for the context and style of music performed.

Objective

- Students will discuss and demonstrate specific behaviors that are appropriate or inappropriate when attending a concert presented by choral musicians from the middle school or a community children's chorus.

Materials

- Transparency with a list of words, similar to the example given in step 1
- Copies of a printed choral program that describes the choir and provides a list of pieces presented at a children's choir concert in the community
- Overhead projector

Prior Knowledge and Experiences

- Students have listened to recorded music in class.
- Some students have attended performances in the community.

Procedures

1. Initiate thinking about concert behavior with this challenge: "Here is a list of words [*show transparency*]. Let's read them all. Which of these words describes your behavior when you are listening to music in your music class?"

   sitting - kneeling - standing - lying down - going to the restroom

   being still - conducting - moving/dancing - nodding your head - keeping the beat on your leg

   being silent - humming - singing - whispering - talking - tapping

   eating - drinking - chewing candy - opening a wrapper (candy, gum, sandwich)

   applauding - whistling - stamping your feet - standing to applaud

2. Ask, "When do you listen to music at home? Are you really listening to the music? What are you doing when you listen to it?" Have students answer from the list of behaviors again.

3. Extend the discussion by asking, for example, "Do you ever go out with your friends or members of your family to places where you listen to music? Where? When? What is the correct behavior for [*name the event*]? Has someone ever told you not to do something at a concert?"

4. Relate the students' comments to other experiences such as those at a place of worship, sports events, indoor or outdoor concerts in the community, or those seen on television.

5. Hand out copies of a printed choral program. Say, "Pretend that you have just arrived at a choir concert and someone at the door gave you a program. What would you do with it? What would you do with your program during the performance of the music? Are there any choral compositions on the program that you have heard of or sung yourself? Have you heard of any of the composers?"

6. Ask students to think of what might have happened at the event described on the program and how the audience would have behaved appropriately.

7. Remind students of the concerts they will attend and discuss when to enter, when to clap, when it is appropriate to talk, and when to get up and leave.

Indicators of Success

- Students behave appropriately at subsequent musical events at school and in the community.

Follow-up

- Encourage students to observe audience behavior at other school or community concerts, especially when they are the performers.
- Reward students for their music achievement by taking them to a community children's chorus concert.

STRATEGIES
Grades 5–8

STANDARD 1A

Singing, alone and with others, a varied repertoire of music: Students sing accurately and with good breath control throughout their singing ranges, alone and in small and large ensembles.

Objective

- Students will sing accurately with good breath control, expressing the text with appropriate dynamics and tempo.

Materials

- Solo or unison legato song with long phrases, such as "Linden Lea" by Ralph Vaughan Williams (New York: Boosey & Hawkes), OCTB6635, unison, Level 1; or "Where'er You Walk" by George Frideric Handel (Toronto: Gordon V. Thompson Music), VG-197, unison, Level 1

Prior Knowledge and Experiences

- Students can sing the selected song.
- Students demonstrate good sitting and standing postures for singing.

Procedures

1. Ask students to roll their shoulders back and down, keeping the chest in a high or level position. Have them place one hand on the upper chest to keep it steady and place the other hand with the thumb at the base of the sternum and the fifth finger on the navel. Demonstrate taking a long, cold air sip and filling the lower hand with air. Invite students to do the same. Ask them to feel the release of the abdominal muscles.

2. Have students maintain hand positions and "hiss" each phrase as the accompaniment for the selected song is played. As you conduct through the phrases, be sure to indicate where students should sip the air, filling the lower hand.

3. Ask students to think the text as the pianist plays the accompaniment in tempo and with dynamics. Challenge them to allow the air to "fall" into the body as they feel each phrase in the body and hear it in the mind.

4. Ask students to sing the song in tempo with dynamics and without accompaniment. Challenge them to continue to feel the breath fill the lower hand and to feel the release of the abdominal muscles.

5. Conduct as the ensemble performs the song with accompaniment. Have students stand in good singing position with hands at sides. Remind them to feel the breath enter the body for each phrase as they sing the song with expression.

Indicators of Success

- Students control the breath to express the text with appropriate dynamics and accurate pitch.

Follow-up

- Add to the chorus's repertoire other songs that have long phrases, such as "Bist du bei mir" by Johann Sebastian Bach (Toronto: Gordon V. Thompson Music), G-183, unison, Level 1.

- Help students continue to develop breath control by including at least one long-phrase song in each rehearsal. Apply procedures in this strategy when teaching such songs.

Singing, alone and with others, a varied repertoire of music: Students sing with expression and technical accuracy a repertoire of vocal literature with a level of difficulty of 2, on a scale of 1 to 6, including some songs performed from memory.

Objective

- Students will sing a composition with a level of difficulty of 2, demonstrating an understanding of the dynamic demands of the score and applying their knowledge of a coding system for the dynamics.

Materials

- Choral octavo such as "The Dove and the Maple Tree" by Antonin Dvorak (Fort Lauderdale, FL: Walton Music Corporation), WH-141, two-part, Level 2

- Set of colored pencils (red, blue, green, brown) for each student

- Teacher-made chart of a color code for analysis:

  Red = *f, ff, sfz, cresc., accel.*

  Blue = *p, pp, dim., rit.*

  Green = *mp*

  Brown = *mf* (also reinforce accents and stress markings in brown)

Prior Knowledge and Experiences

- Students can follow their own vocal lines in a choral score and identify the part for other voices.

Procedures

1. Distribute a choral octavo to each singer. Talk through the color coding system with students, and ask for examples of places in the score where they will mark red, blue, green, and brown. When students have grasped the concept, have them mark the first page of the score, color coding the expressive markings (see Materials). Before students go on to finish the score, scan their first pages to be sure they are marking the music correctly. Then have them finish color coding the piece.

2. After the score is marked, lead students to discover the range of dynamics used by the composer, arranger, or editor in the score as a whole.

3. Invite students to recite the text in rhythm with dynamics. Ask for volunteers to point out repeated words and phrases. Help students discover how the composer, arranger, or editor heard the text by speaking it again with correct dynamics and with careful attention to repeated text and phrases.

4. Conduct students in singing the composition with understanding of dynamics indicated by the composer, arranger, or editor.

Indicators of Success

- Students perform the selected piece with sensitivity to the expressive markings, especially the dynamic markings, that they have marked in the score.

Follow-up

- Have students apply the same procedure for marking and analyzing their scores as a regular part of the process of learning future choral works in class.

- Help students extend the markings, including reinforcing the ending bar lines of major sections of the piece in black, and labeling sections using letters such as A and B or other appropriate labels to help them discover the form of the music.

Singing, alone and with others, a varied repertoire of music: Students sing with expression and technical accuracy a repertoire of vocal literature with a difficulty level of 2, on a scale of 1 to 6, including some songs performed from memory.

Objective

- Students will sing a contemporary composition with a level of difficulty of 2, identifying compositional techniques used by the composer to convey the meaning of the text, including expressive markings and meter changes.

Materials

- "Under My Command" by Mary Goetze (New York: Boosey & Hawkes), OCTB6765, two-part, Level 2

Prior Knowledge and Experiences

- Students have sung music in two parts and in 2/4 and 6/8 meters.
- Students have studied expressive markings indicating tempo and dynamics.

Procedures

1. Ask students to read silently the poem in the Treble I part and decide where the text changes from "reality" to "fantasy." Ask students to look for references from books they have read. Some students may be able to identify the references to *Gulliver's Travels* and *Twenty Thousand Leagues Under the Sea.*

2. As students listen to you sing the Treble I part, have them follow the score and identify compositional techniques that help convey the drama of the text (for example, dramatic contrasts in dynamics, changes in tempo, an aleatoric section, changes in meter, changes in voice quality).

3. Ask students to identify the dynamic level and sing the fantasy theme at measures 5–10 and then identify the place that the theme reappears either exactly in the same form or in a variation. [*It reappears at measure 35, this time in 6/8 meter.*] Challenge students to identify the new meter signature and then to speak the text in the new rhythm, making certain to notice the change from a feeling of two beats per measure to three beats per measure at measure 38. Rehearse both parts from measures 35–49.

4. Ask students to sing the opening motive at the correct dynamic level. Lead them to discover where this motive appears again [*measures 51–55*], and have students sing those measures.

5. Ask students to clap the melodic rhythm in the Treble I part, measures 14–31, and then sing those measures at the correct dynamic level, making sure to change the timbre of their voices at measures 23 and 26. Repeat this process with the Treble II part, and then have students sing both parts together. Rehearse the glissando at measures 14–15, allowing time for students to come in at their own rate, as indicated by the composer.

6. Invite students to sing the song from the beginning, paying close attention to the dynamic and metric changes in the score.

(continued)

Indicators of Success

- Students accurately identify dynamic, meter, and tempo changes in the selected song and artistically perform the song with the expressiveness indicated in the musical score.

- Students relate the composer's use of expressive markings and meter changes to the demands of the text.

Follow-up

- Select a poem of great appeal to students, and challenge them to suggest expressive markings for parts of the text. Give students at least two choices of tempo or meter, and let them create a rhythm for the text. Have students read the text with their choices of rhythm, tempo, and dynamics.

- Have students create a suitable melody for a text they have set to rhythm.

Singing, alone and with others, a varied repertoire of music: Students sing music representing diverse genres and cultures, with expression appropriate for the work being performed.

Objective

- Students will sing a South African freedom song with appropriate expression and style, incorporating appropriate hand-clapping and body movements typical of those used by South African singers.

Materials

- "Freedom Is Coming," collected by Anders Nyberg, ed. Henry H. Leck (Fort Lauderdale, FL: Walton Music Corporation), WW1149, three-part, Level 2; WW1174, SAB, Level 2

- Audiocassette recording of "Freedom Is Coming," Walton Music Corporation, 44WB528C

- Audiocassette player

- *Graceland* by Paul Simon, Warner Reprise Video 338136 (optional)

- Videocassette recorder and video monitor (if videotape is used)

Procedures

1. Teach the song "Freedom Is Coming" to the chorus, identifying it as a freedom song from South Africa.

2. Lead a discussion in which students draw parallels between signal songs from the slavery period, Civil Rights protest songs from the 1960s, and songs of the South African anti-apartheid movement.

3. After students can sing the vocal parts of "Freedom Is Coming" together, add hand-clapping and body movements appropriate to South African music. If *Graceland* videotape is available, show students selected portions so that they can see how South African musicians incorporate movement into musical performance.

   Select clapping techniques from the following:

   a. Clap hands together on beats 1 and 2; pat/clap hands of the person on either side on beats 3 and 4.

   b. Hold hands slightly to the side and front of the body, with right hand palm up, left hand palm down; on beats 1 and 2, bring hands into contact with those of the person on either side, reversing palm position on the second beat (left palm up, right palm down); clap hands in front of the body on beats 3 and 4.

   Select body movements from the following:

   a. Lightly step in left-right-left-left, right-left-right-right pattern throughout the song.

   b. Using the above light stepping pattern, move gradually forward, then back to the original position as often as directed.

4. As the chorus continues to prepare the music, review the appropriate performance style by questioning, by students' assessment of their performance, and by comparison with the *Graceland* video if the students have seen it.

Indicators of Success

- Students appropriately identify authentic South African style of performance and body movements and apply it to their own performance of "Freedom Is Coming."

(continued)

Prior Knowledge and Experiences

- Some students have studied the period of the American Civil War, the American Civil Rights Movement of the 1960s, and apartheid in South Africa in other classes.

- Some students can define "signal song" and "freedom song."

Follow-up

- After videotaping the students' performance in concert, show them the videotape, and ask them whether they performed the vocal style and movements in a style matching the South African performance characteristics they discussed or viewed.

- Help students extend their repertoire of choral experiences by having them perform a variety of styles in American music, such as Black gospel, jazz, and blues. A number of choral arrangements in these styles suitable for young singers are available through Boosey & Hawkes; for example, for Black History Month, see songs arranged by Barbara Baker (New York: Boosey & Hawkes).

Singing, alone and with others, a varied repertoire of music: Students sing music representing diverse genres and cultures, with expression appropriate for the work being performed.

Objective

- Students will perform repertoire of three or more different styles, using appropriate expression and stylistic variation.

Materials

- Octavo in a distinctive vocal style, such as: "Mary Had a Little Blues" by Charles Collins (New York: Boosey & Hawkes), OCTB6758, two-part, Level 2; "Bye Oh Baby," arr. Malcolm Dalglish (New York: Boosey & Hawkes), OCTB6633, two-part, Level 2; "Feel Good," arr. Barbara Baker and David Elliott (New York: Boosey & Hawkes), OCTB6711, SSA, Level 2; "Dodo Li," arr. Doreen Rao (New York: Boosey & Hawkes), OCTB6679, unison, Level 1; "Hymn To Freedom" by Oscar Peterson (Fort Lauderdale, FL: Walton Music Corporation), WW1135, SSA, Level 3; "Nukapianguaq" (Inuit chants), arr. Stephen Hatfield (New York: Boosey & Hawkes), OCTB6700, four-part (mostly unison/two-part), Level 2; or "Niška Banja," arr. Nick Page (New York: Boosey & Hawkes), OCTB6517, SAAB or SSAA, Level 2

Procedures

1. Invite students to listen to three or more examples of authentic vocal performances such as Black gospel music or Appalachian folk music. Ask students to listen for use of such aspects as language and vocalization, vocal tone, relationship to accompaniment, dynamic range, and rhythmic interpretation.

2. Ask students to describe characteristics of the various styles. List on the chalkboard the characteristics of each style for reference and comparison. If students cannot verbalize their descriptions, ask them to demonstrate what they mean with their voices.

3. Apply the students' knowledge of vocal style to the performance piece you have selected. Ask, "How should the voice sound in this style?" Guide students to examine the entire octavo and discover what the composer or arranger has written that will give them clues to a stylistic vocalization of the song. Again, if they do not have all the vocabulary they need to describe vocalization in the style, have them demonstrate their description with their voices.

4. Using the selected piece, invite students to experiment with appropriate techniques for the selected song, such as scat singing, scooping with the voice, bending pitches, or other stylistic techniques. Lead them to explore various vowel colors that are heard in the recorded examples; for example, singing the vowels brighter or darker (more forward or farther back in the mouth), with lips more rounded or more widely spread, or with more or less nasal quality.

5. Ask students to compare their performance to a vocal recording in the style of their piece. Help them evaluate how stylistically authentic their performance sounds.

Indicators of Success

- Students demonstrate through choral performance the ability to express appropriately a variety of musical styles.

(continued)

- Recordings of authentic music that represents the various styles of the octavos listed: blues, southern Appalachian, Black gospel, Israeli, jazz, Inuit, and Serbian
- Audio-playback equipment
- Chalkboard

Prior Knowledge and Experiences

- Students can identify various singing styles such as country, pop, classical, and rock.
- Students can describe vocal qualities and styles such as nasal-sounding, ornamented, legato, and twangy and can explain, by example, such techniques as scooping, bending pitches, laid-back rhythm, and scat singing.

Follow-up

- Introduce a piece to the chorus that is in a style that is somewhat new to you. In a cooperative project with the students, seek out sources of authority—recordings, videotapes, and choral directors with experience in performing a variety of styles—to foster an authentic performance of the new piece.

STANDARD 1D

Singing, alone and with others, a varied repertoire of music:
Students sing music written in two and three parts.

Objective

- Students will sing a one-octave scale in a two-part round, using a variety of rhythm patterns.

Materials

- Keyboard (for pitches only)

Prior Learning and Experiences

- Students are able to sing unison songs as a group.

Procedures

1. Ask students to sing a scale (C major or D major), using numbers or solfège syllables. Then ask students to repeat the scale, singing each pitch as four quarter notes. Allow them to count the four quarter notes on their fingers as they sing them.

2. Direct students to repeat the scale, singing each pitch as two half notes. Have students count the four beats of the two half notes on their fingers as they sing them.

3. Have students repeat the scale, singing each pitch as four quarter notes while ascending the octave, then as two half notes when descending. Tell students that they may continue to count the patterns on their fingers as they sing them.

4. Divide the class into two groups—Group 1 and Group 2. Have Group 1 begin its scale using quarter notes. When Group 1 gets to the third tone of the scale, direct Group 2 to begin its scale. Since Group 1 will finish first, have it continue to repeat the first pitch of the scale until Group 2 finishes its scale. Switch the order of the groups and ask students to sing the scales again.

5. Use the exercise to progress to higher keys, encouraging use of the head voice.

6. As students progress in their ability to sing the exercise well, have them repeat it using half notes, then combinations of rhythm patterns.

Indicators of Success

- Students sing an ascending, then descending, scale in a round, learning to sing in harmony.

Follow-up

- Divide students into three groups and have them sing rounds in three parts. Then expand to more parts.

STANDARD 1E

Singing, alone and with others, a varied repertoire of music: Students sing with expression and technical accuracy a varied repertoire of vocal literature with a level of difficulty of 3, on a scale of 1 to 6, including some songs performed from memory.

Objective

- After a thorough analysis of the text, students will sing a two-part a cappella piece, with a level of difficulty of 3, in an expressive, musical manner.

Materials

- "The Cuckoo, the Nightingale, and the Donkey" by Gustav Mahler (New York: Oxford University Press), 82.075, SA, Level 3

Prior Knowledge and Experiences

- Students have sung "The Cuckoo, the Nightingale, and the Donkey" in rehearsal, and they can recognize the vocal parts as they look at the score.

- Students can sing two-part a cappella music.

- Students can read a score, follow dynamic markings, and identify systems and measures.

Procedures

1. Conduct as students perform "The Cuckoo, the Nightingale, and the Donkey" with piano accompaniment. Direct students' attention to proper posture and breath support.

2. Ask students to scan the text and discover who the characters are. (Do not leave out the narrator.) Ask, "Who is speaking in the first eight measures of the vocal parts? Where do you first hear the voice of the nightingale singing alone?" Have students answer by page, system, and measure, or by word in the text. "What characteristic of the part convinces you that it is the nightingale that is singing?" Invite students to perform that section after it is discovered. Have students sing on "ng" so that the pitches will carry with a fuller, more resonant sound.

3. Ask students, "Where do you first hear the cuckoo warming up?" Have students sing the cuckoo's warm-up after they discover it. Ask students whether they should sing the voice of the cuckoo in the same manner as the voice of the nightingale. Direct singers' attention to the staccato markings. If they sing "cuckoo" incorrectly, sing it for them once legato and once staccato. Ask students to tell you which way of singing is indicated in the music. Then have them perform it correctly.

4. Conduct students as they perform the piece from the beginning to page 2, system 4, measure 4.

5. Ask students, "In what measure do we discover why the birds want the donkey to be the judge?" Have them sing, "For since he has two great big ears, great big ears, great big ears." Direct particular attention to their dynamics when they perform this section. If the difference on repeated parts is not marked enough, sing it once with no dynamic contrast, then sing it again with much contrast (whisper the second "great big ears" as if you are telling a secret to a friend). Ask students to tell you which way is indicated in the music, and then have them perform it again with correct dynamics.

6. Have students sing the piece from the beginning through page 3, system 4, measure 4. Ask students to identify the place in the score in which each creature takes a turn in the competition. Have them perform each creature's section as it is discovered. Ask students, "Why did the donkey believe the cuckoo should win the prize?" Have students perform the donkey's verdict with proper dynamics. Have students give you two reasons why they know the donkey has the last word. [*The donkey is the judge, and "hee haw" is the last word in the song!*]

7. Conduct as students perform the entire piece, expressing the text as meaningfully as possible as they sing.

Indicators of Success

■ Students "sing their understanding" of the text of "The Cuckoo, the Nightingale, and the Donkey" in an expressive, musical manner.

■ Each character in the text is distinguishable through the students' performance.

Follow-up

■ Teach students another piece that offers opportunity for unique textual analysis and expression, such as "O Captain, My Captain" by Elam Sprenkle, with text by Walt Whitman (New York: Boosey & Hawkes), OCTB6644, SS, Level 3.

STANDARD 2A

Performing on instruments, alone and with others, a varied repertoire of music: Students perform on at least one instrument accurately and independently, alone and in small and large ensembles, with good posture, good playing position, and good breath, bow, or stick control.

Objective

- Students will demonstrate basic techniques for playing nonpitched percussion instruments in an ensemble rondo piece.

Materials

- Percussion instruments such as claves, bongos, guiro, cowbell, and hand drums

Prior Knowledge and Experiences

- Students can read and perform simple rhythm patterns.
- Students have worked with rondo form.

Procedures

1. Identify names and timbres of selected percussion instruments by demonstrating simple rhythmic patterns. (Invite a percussion specialist to visit your classroom, or become one!)

2. Demonstrate:

claves—Curl left-hand fingers loosely into a "hot dog bun," and lay one clave lightly on top. Be sure there is open space under the clave for resonance. Hold second clave lightly in the right hand at an angle. Strike the center of the clave with a rebound. Typical Cuban clave rhythm is:

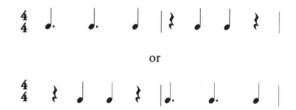

guiro—Hold the opening or "mouth" toward the audience and the "tail" toward the performer's body. Place the thumb and index finger in the holes. Hold the thicker part of the scraper with the right hand. Use down-and-up scrapes. Basic guiro rhythm: One long scrape, followed by two short scrapes or taps.

cowbell—Lay the cowbell on the left-hand palm with the open "mouth" to the audience. Play with the stick across the rim of the mouth or with the stick tapping the closed end. For a louder sound, hold the bell with the left-hand fingertips. [*Note:* A good player is needed on cowbell in order to get the best sound from the instrument.]

bongos—If there is no stand, grip the instrument between the knees and slightly tilt the drums away from the body. Position the smaller drum head, the "lead drum," closest to the dominant hand. Play on the edge of the skin with one or two inches of middle and/or index finger. Practice syncopated rhythms.

hand drum—Hold the drum with the left hand in front of the body as if shaking hands. Play the drum with the right hand (or dominant hand) using three middle fingers. Strike at ten-o'clock position near the rim with brush strokes upward and away from body. Alternate technique for accents or faster tempo; use the thumb with a downward-away motion at the four-o'clock position.

3. Divide students into groups of no more than five with the stated goal of creating a percussion ensemble rondo piece. Ask students to compose a four-measure rhythm pattern in 4/4 meter for each instrument using previously learned rhythms. Have them practice rhythms with clapping or body percussion and transfer the rhythms to the specific instruments.

4. Have students perform composed four-measure patterns together as the A section of the rondo. Allow a student on each instrument to take a turn at improvising the other four-measure sections (for example, B = guiro, C = cowbell, and so forth).

Indicators of Success

■ Students successfully perform a percussion rhythm ensemble, demonstrating appropriate basic instrumental techniques and rondo form.

Follow-up

■ Have students create instrumental ostinatos to accompany Carribean songs; for example, "Tinga Layo," in *Share the Music,* Grade 2 (New York: Macmillan/McGraw-Hill, 1995); *Music and You,* Grade 3 (New York: Macmillan/McGraw-Hill, 1991); or *World of Music,* Grade 3 (Parsippany, NJ: Silver Burdett Ginn, 1991).

STANDARD 2B

Performing on instruments, alone and with others, a varied repertoire of music: Students perform with expression and technical accuracy on at least one string, wind, percussion, or classroom instrument a repertoire of instrumental literature with a level of difficulty of 2, on a scale of 1 to 6.

Objective

- Students will demonstrate choral phrasing and expression in a stringed instrument arrangement of a Mozart piece with a level of difficulty of 2.

Materials

- Choral scores for "Ave Verum Corpus" by Wolfgang Amadeus Mozart (Chapel Hill, NC: Hinshaw Music), HMC-490, SATB, Level 2

- String scores for Mozart's "Ave Verum Corpus" (Chapel Hill, NC: Hinshaw Music)

Prior Knowledge and Experiences

- Using good playing position, students can produce a good tone on a violin, viola, or cello.

- Students have studied basic notes, scales, and bowings on violin, viola, or cello.

- Students can sing Mozart's "Ave Verum Corpus" with good choral sound and appropriate style.

Procedures

1. After they sing through "Ave Verum Corpus," ask students to focus on the phrases. Encourage them to discover phrase lengths. Review the concept of phrasing and how phrases should be shaped in this piece.

2. Have students sing the first two phrases of the song, paying close attention to phrase shape. Discuss the concept of breath support to carry through a phrase.

3. Have students on stringed instruments (violin I, violin II, viola, cello) play each line of the first two phrases alone (voice parts).

4. Ask the class to evaluate the shape of each phrase and make suggestions for improvement.

5. Repeat steps 3 and 4 several times, as needed, with the same phrases.

6. Choose a small ensemble of strings to accompany the rest of the class's singing of the first two phrases. Then have the singers perform the phrases with string accompaniment.

Indicators of Success

- Students effectively shape phrases using proper dynamics while playing and singing the first two phrases of "Ave Verum Corpus."

Follow-up

- Have a small ensemble of exceptional string players accompany the choir for a performance of "Ave Verum Corpus."

STANDARD 2C

Performing on instruments, alone and with others, a varied repertoire of music: Students perform music representing diverse genres and cultures, with expression appropriate for the work being performed.

Objective

- Students will accompany on pitched and nonpitched percussion instruments a song from the repertoire in a style appropriate to the work.

Materials

- Piece from students' choral repertoire representing another culture or style, such as a folk song or a calypso

- Recording of pieces in a style similar to that of the selected piece

- Pitched and/or nonpitched percussion instruments

- Audio-playback equipment

Prior Knowledge and Experiences

- Students have studied and performed as an ensemble songs from other cultures and genres.

- Students have experience playing classroom percussion instruments such as guiro, claves, castanets, triangle, cowbell, and wood block.

Procedures

1. Review with students a song from their repertoire that is from another culture or genre.

2. Play recordings of pieces in a style similar to the selected piece.

3. Discuss styles and, if possible, demonstrate instruments commonly used to accompany the style; for example: claves in Brazilian samba music; castanets in Argentinian tango music.

4. Ask students, through listening and singing, to develop appropriate accompaniment figures/ostinatos for the piece.

5. Help students rehearse ostinatos, adjusting them to fit the overall form of the song.

6. Have students perform the song. After a successful performance, have students switch parts, switch between singing and playing, or both.

Indicators of Success

- Students accurately perform appropriate accompaniment patterns to songs from another culture or genre.

Follow-up

- Have students investigate in depth the instruments of another culture, perhaps having them make their own instruments.

- Guide students in an analysis of the similarities and differences between songs representing two or more cultures.

STANDARD 2D

Performing on instruments, alone and with others, a varied repertoire of music:
*Students play by ear simple melodies on a melodic instrument and simple
accompaniments on a harmonic instrument.*

Objectives

- Students will echo a simple two-measure melody using a soprano recorder, harmonize the melody using pitched classroom instruments, and combine the melody and harmony to create a homophonic composition.

Materials

- "Cockles and Mussels," Irish folk song (transposed to G if necessary), in *Folksong Encyclopedia,* Volume 1, arr. Silverman (Milwaukee: Hal Leonard Corporation, 1981)
- Soprano recorders
- Pitched classroom instruments such as metallophones, glockenspiels, or xylophones (using only tonic, subdominant, and dominant bars)
- Audiocassette recorder, microphone, and blank tape

Prior Knowledge and Experiences

- Students have experience with proper mallet techniques and have used classroom instruments in various choral and instrumental settings.
- On soprano recorders, students can play from notation the range of a twelfth.

Procedures

1. Stand in the back of the classroom so that students will not see your recorder fingering, tell students the starting pitch, and then play a simple one-measure melodic pattern on the recorder (in 4/4 meter) using three pitches. Have students imitate the correct pitch and rhythm of the melodic pattern. Using two additional pitches, gradually expand the melody to two measures of 4/4 meter with a rest on beat eight. [*Note:* The first measure should be built around the tonic, and the second around the subdominant.]

2. Instruct half the class to move to pitched classroom instruments to play an accompaniment following the chord symbols for the first two measures of the song "Cockles and Mussels." Give students some time to experiment softly on the instruments, tapping their fingers on the bars to ascertain the correct accompaniment pitches. Conducting in 4/4 meter, have students play beats one and three on the correct bars using mallets.

3. Have the recorder group playing the melody join those playing the accompaniment instruments and rehearse the song. Record the work as the class performs it.

4. Have students switch parts, with those students on recorder moving to accompaniment instruments. Reteach the recorder melody by aural imitation (students hear the melody and echo the pattern). Then record the class again on their new parts.

Indicators of Success

- Students imitate the melody on soprano recorder with correct pitches and rhythm.
- Students harmonize the melody with chords played on pitched classroom instruments.
- Students perform the melody or harmony with an ensemble.

Follow-up

- After students have learned the song "Cockles and Mussels," have them imitate its melody on the recorders and accompany the song on pitched classroom instruments using notes from the three chords in the accompaniment.

STANDARD 2E

Performing on instruments, alone and with others, a varied repertoire of music: Students perform with expression and technical accuracy a varied repertoire of instrumental literature with a level of difficulty of 3, on a scale of 1 to 6, including some solos performed from memory.

Objective

- Students will perform with expression and technical accuracy an accompaniment, with a level of difficulty of 3, to an octavo on a selected instrument.

Materials

- Choral works accompanied by:

  ukelele—"Li'l Lisa Jane," TTBB, Level 2, in *Barbershop Memories,* compiled H. Frey (Miami: Warner Bros. Publications, 1984)

  handbells—"A Jubilant Song" by Allen Pote (Carol Stream, IL: Hope Publishing Company), F979, SACB, Level 2; "Ding, Dong, Merrily on High," arr. G. A. Smith (Nashville: Broadman Press), 4561-05, SAB, Level 2; or "Beautiful Star" by Libby Larson (Boston: E. C. Schirmer), 4202, SACB, Level 2

  xylophones—"Children's Praise" by Ronald Nelson (Garland, TX: Choristers Guild), CGA-5764, unison, Level 1

  guitars—"Gift to Be Simple," arr. M. Pooler (New York: G. Schirmer), 11869, SAT/CB, Level 2

Procedures

1. Tell students that each of them is going to learn to play an instrument well enough to accompany one of the songs that they have been learning to sing. Review vocal parts of the selected songs.

2. Introduce students to the various instruments and the musical task, making the initial focus on technical accuracy on the instrument. Encourage experienced students to help instruct the less-experienced through informal mentoring or peer teaching.

3. Assign each student to a specific ensemble for final rehearsals.

4. Combine instrumental accompaniments with voices and have students perform the pieces.

Indicators of Success

- Students perform instrumental accompaniment parts for the selected choral octavos with technical accuracy.

Follow-up

- Once students can perform with technical accuracy, have them produce a videotape of each student rehearsing and performing his or her assigned instrument within the ensemble, focusing on expressive elements. Allow students to study and to discuss the videotapes, offering constructive feedback when appropriate.

- Have students perform the selected works with student instrumental accompaniment (either live or through a presentation of the videotapes) for parents or other classes.

- Lead a discussion of the similarities and differences between instruments used in a given lesson and the voice.

- Invite a brass quartet to perform Allen Pote's "A Jubilant Song" with your students. Discuss pros and cons of combining the brass timbre and volume with the other instruments students have been playing.

(continued)

- Ukeleles

- Handbells

- Xylophones

- Guitars

- Piano or electronic keyboard

[*Note:* Levels in Materials indicate levels of difficulty of the choral parts.]

Prior Knowledge and Experiences

- Students have sung numerous unison songs as part of an ensemble.

- Students have been rehearsing vocal parts of the songs selected for Procedures.

STANDARD 3A

Improvising melodies, variations, and accompaniments: Students improvise simple harmonic accompaniments.

Objectives

- Students will improvise an accompaniment to a given melody vocally and on pitched classroom instruments using tonic, subdominant, and dominant chord tones.

Materials

- Pitched classroom instruments such as glockenspiels, xylophones, and metallophones
- Chalkboard
- Charts with prepared melodic examples

Prior Knowledge and Experiences

- Students can play simple melodies in pentatonic, modal, and diatonic keys on pitched classroom instruments.
- Students have studied the structure of tonic, subdominant, and dominant chords and have demonstrated their knowledge of these chords through vocal exercises.

Procedures

1. During vocal exercises, play the tonic *do* on the keyboard and have students harmonize the pitch with a tonic chord (sopranos on *sol,* altos on *mi,* and cambiata voices on *do*). Move to the second scale degree, and have students adjust to harmonize a dominant chord (sopranos remain on *sol,* altos down to *re,* cambiatas down to *ti*). Continue through a major diatonic scale, having the singers adjust their pitches accordingly.

2. Play a simple melody on the keyboard (such as *sol, fa, mi, fa, sol, mi, do*), and map the melody on the chalkboard for the students. Have students decide how to vocally harmonize the melody using the tonic, subdominant, and dominant chords, and determine which scale degree of the initial chord they will start on. Then have them sing the I-IV-V chords in the harmonic structure, one chord at a time.

3. Have students repeat the completed harmonic structure, adding the correct melodic rhythm. Then have them repeat the harmony while you play or sing the melody.

4. Have half the students sit in front of the pitched classroom instruments. Present a four-measure melody in 4/4 meter that you have prepared on a chart. Have remaining students sightread the melody using solfège syllables while students at the instruments accompany the melody by playing either tonic, subdominant, or dominant chords on beats 1 and 3 of each measure. Repeat the pattern until both groups are successful.

5. Have students switch places and present a new melody on a chart.

Indicators of Success

- Using tonic, subdominant, and dominant chords, students vocally improvise an accompaniment to a given melody.
- Using tonic, subdominant, and dominant chords, students improvise on pitched classroom instruments an accompaniment to a given melody.

(continued)

Follow-up

- Introduce the Brazilian folk song "Sambalelê," in *Share the Music,* Grade 1, teacher's edition (New York: Macmillan/McGraw-Hill, 1995). Have students improvise a rhythmic accompaniment using the tonic, subdominant, and dominant chords on pitched classroom instruments, as well as improvise vocally over the chordal accompaniment, using the root of the chord as their tonal center.

STANDARD 3B

Improvising melodies, variations, and accompaniments: Students improvise melodic embellishments and simple rhythmic and melodic variations on given pentatonic melodies and melodies in major keys.

Objective

- Students will improvise Baroque ornamentation on the repeated A section of a da capo aria.

Materials

- "Where'er You Walk" by George Frideric Handel (Toronto: Gordon V. Thompson Music), VG-197, unison, Level 1
- Chart with labeled examples of (a) appoggiatura; (b) mordent; (c) and inverted mordent (see step 3)

Prior Knowledge and Experiences

- As a chorus, students can sing correct pitches and rhythms in "Where'er You Walk."

Procedures

1. Review "Where'er You Walk" by having the chorus sing it with good posture, breath control, tone quality, and diction.

2. Model the first phrase, "Where'er you walk, cool gales shall fan the glade," using an appoggiatura on the beat on the words "walk" and "glade." Sing the appoggiatura on the beat as follows:

Wher- e'er you walk,   cool gales shall fan the glade;

3. Challenge students to identify (a, b, or c) which type of ornament you used in singing the phrase by looking at the chart with the following examples and listening to you sing the phrase with the appoggiaturas again:

(a) appoggiatura   (b) mordent   (c) inverted mordent

Ask, "Which type of ornament did I use? How did you know it was an appoggiatura?"

4. Ask, "Can one of you sing the phrase 'Trees where you sit' and put an appoggiatura on the word 'sit'?"

5. Using the song "Where'er You Walk," model a mordent or inverted mordent, singing the ornamentation on the beat. Have students identify the ornament from the chart. Again ask, "How do you know? Suggest that someone sing that phrase (or another one) using a mordent or inverted mordent in another place. Try the same process with other volunteers, instructing them to sing the ornament on the beat.

(continued)

6. Divide the chorus into three sections. Ask students in each section to individually and collectively explore ways to sing the first page with ornamentation (about five minutes). Caution them about excessive use of ornamentation. Have them decide as a section which ornaments to use on the phrase and to sing their version for the other choristers. Then have students decide as a chorus on a way to ornament the whole da capo A section.

7. Have students perform the whole piece with unornamented A and B sections and with an ornamented da capo A section.

Indicators of Success

- Students sing examples of the types of ornaments that they choose in places in the da capo A section, demonstrating their understanding in the act of improvising the ornaments.

- Students make decisions about the types of ornament to be sung on particular notes.

- Students perform examples of Baroque music with stylistically appropriate use of improvisation.

Follow-up

- Have students learn and perform other Baroque da capo pieces with ornamentation in the da capo A section; for example, "Art Thou Troubled?" by G. F. Handel (Delaware Water Gap, PA: Novello/Shawnee Press), 1038, unison, Level 1.

STANDARD 3C

Improvising melodies, variations, and accompaniments: Students improvise short melodies, unaccompanied and over given rhythmic accompaniments, each in a consistent style, meter, and tonality.

Objectives

- Students will sing tonic, subdominant, and dominant chords within a vocal ensemble and improvise an antecedent/consequent melodic phrase with melodic intervals up to a major sixth.

Materials

- Chalkboard, or chart, with staff lines
- Audiocassette recorder, microphone, and blank tape

Prior Knowledge and Experiences

- Students have studied the structure of tonic, subdominant, and dominant triads (major and minor) and are able to harmonize vocally in three parts.
- Students have experimented with melodic improvisation using intervals no larger than a major third.

Procedures

1. During vocal exercises, assign each student a pitch of the tonic triad. Using fingers, indicate the triad to which students should move (either subdominant or dominant). Have students make appropriate adjustments by either raising or lowering their pitch one scale degree or remaining on the same pitch.

2. Review improvising a four-measure antecedent/consequent phrase using intervals no larger than a third. Demonstrate a four-measure phrase using a variety of intervals no larger than a sixth. Have students imitate your melodic improvisation. Then, have them translate the improvisation to solfège and map the melody on the chalkboard. Lead students in a harmonization of the melody using I, IV, and V triads.

3. Have the class divide into groups of two to improvise a melody using intervals up to a major sixth. Ask each pair of students to present its improvisation to the ensemble as you tape each presentation.

4. After all students have presented and the improvisations have been recorded, have students choose three to map and harmonize. Write the three chosen melodies on the chalkboard. Then have students as a group decide on the harmonization for each melody and rehearse the results.

5. Record the final presentations of the works as the students perform them.

Indicators of Success

- Students sing tonic, subdominant, and dominant chords within a vocal ensemble.
- Students improvise an antecedent/consequent melodic phrase, and incorporate melodic intervals up to a major sixth.

(continued)

Follow-up

- Have students sing the round "By the Rivers of Babylon" by Lowell Mason, ed. Salli Terri, Level 1, in *Round America* (New York: Lawson-Gould Music Publishers/G. Schirmer, 1976), LG 51945. Divide the ensemble into two groups, having one group sing melody only and one group improvise the harmony.

- Have students sing the same round in parts, with a few students providing vocal harmonization.

STANDARD 4A

Composing and arranging music within specified guidelines: Students compose short pieces within specified guidelines, demonstrating how the elements of music are used to achieve unity and variety, tension and release, and balance.

Objective

- Students will create and perform a composition using rhythms and/or melodic instrumental motives to match characters, events, and places in a reading.

Materials

- Selected story for oral presentation

- Classroom percussion instruments, including glockenspiel, metallophone, xylophone, timpani, claves, maracas, wood block, temple blocks, conga drum, tambourine, triangle, gong, rhythm sticks, sand block, cabaça, and castanets

Prior Knowledge and Experiences

- Students can demonstrate correct playing technique of classroom percussion instruments.

- Students can discern timbres of classroom percussion instruments.

- Students have experience improvising rhythmic ostinatos and melodies on instruments.

- Students have experience with vocal improvisation.

Procedures

1. Before they hear an oral presentation of the selected story, ask students to be thinking, as they hear the story, about what instrument(s), including voice and body percussion, would be appropriate for a character, place, or event in the story. Read or have a student read the story to the students.

2. After students have heard the story, have them decide on appropriate instruments for characters, events, and places in the plot. Once these decisions have been made, give students appropriate time to experiment with their instruments and create rhythmic or melodic patterns suitable for the length of the event for which they are required to play.

3. Have students add voice and body percussion to the composition.

4. Have students rehearse the entire created "sound" story, adding musical instruments and voice and body percussion in the appropriate places.

5. After students have become more consistent in playing their composition, select a student conductor who is familiar with the reading to cue the ensemble at the appropriate moment in the story.

Indicators of Success

- Students create rhythms and perform a composition using rhythmic and melodic instrumental motives to match characters, events, and places in the selected reading.

- Students reproduce their composition in a consistent form.

Follow-up

- Have students perform their composition with the reading for their peers in a language arts class.

- Have students dramatize the story used in Procedures. Then have them perform the dramatization with their composition.

- Have students take an existing song—such as "My Home So Far Away," arr. Lois R. Land, text by Sally Monsour (Alliance Music Publications, PO Box 131977, Houston, TX 77219-1977; telephone 713-868-9980), AMC1005, two-part, Level 1—and, using instruments and body percussion, enhance the story in the song.

STANDARD 4B

Composing and arranging music within specified guidelines: Students arrange simple pieces for voices or instruments other than those for which the pieces were written.

Objective

- Students will create a rondo arrangement of three calypso-type songs.

Materials

- "Jamaican Market Place" by Larry Farrow (Tarzana, CA: Gentry Publications), J62092, Level 3

- "Mango Walk" (a Jamaican folk song), arr. Brent Pierce (Fort Lauderdale, FL: Plymouth Music Company), BP-402, SAB, Level 2

- "Jamaica Farewell" (a traditional calypso from West Indies), Level 1, in *The Musical Classroom: Backgrounds, Models, and Skills for Elementary Teaching,* 4th ed., by Patricia Hackett and Carolynn A. Lindeman (Englewood Cliffs, NJ: Prentice-Hall, 1997)

- Guitar or chorded zither (such as Autoharp or ChromAharp)

Prior Knowledge and Experiences

- Students can sing the selected calypso-type songs.

- Students can play I, IV, and V7 chords in the key of D on guitar or Autoharp/ChromAharp. Students have studied rondo form.

Procedures

1. Tell the class that together, they will review three previously learned songs. Lead the class in unison singing of the refrain from "Jamaican Market Place," the opening melody from "Mango Walk," and the verse and refrain from "Jamaica Farewell," having selected students accompany the songs on the Autoharp/ChromAharp or guitar in the key of D using D, G, A7 (I, IV, V7) chords.

2. Lead a discussion about phrases and chord structure and how these affect a composition or an arrangement. Continue with a discussion of the elements of arranging, such as chord progressions, continuity of melody, length of sections, similar or contrasting sections, and text.

3. Have the class create arrangements of the three songs in rondo form (ABACA) by dividing the class into small groups and having each group create its own recurring A section from phrases or sections of the three songs.

4. Depending on students' level of experience, explain that they may augment their sections with accompaniment on Autoharp/ChromAharp or guitar, rhythm instruments, or vocal harmonies.

5. Have each group perform its arrangement for the rest of the class.

Indicators of Success

- Students create simple rondo arrangements using three known compositions.

Follow-up

- Have students create rondo arrangements of folk songs in their repertoire on a specific theme; for example, transportation—"This Train," "The Wabash Cannonball," "Michael, Row the Boat Ashore," and "Riding in the Buggy."

STANDARD 4C

Composing and arranging music within specified guidelines: Students use a variety of traditional and nontraditional sound sources and electronic media when composing and arranging.

Objective

- Students will create a composition using synthesized sounds and nontraditional use of traditional instruments including the voice.

Materials

- *In the Beginning* by Daniel Pinkham (Boston: E. C. Schirmer), SATB (ECS 2902) and audiocassette recording of electronic sounds (ECS 2902A), Level 3

- "Rondes" by Folke Rabe (Ft. Lauderdale, FL: Walton Music Corporation), WH-171, SATB, Level 3

- Recordings of any works by John Cage and Karlheinz Stockhausen (Walton Music Corporation; order from Plymouth Music Company, Fort Lauderdale, FL)

- Audiocassette player, microphone, and blank tape

- Compact disc player

- Electronic keyboards and synthesizers

- Various types of sound-makers, such as percussion instruments and found instruments

Procedures

1. Have students listen to one or two examples of the works of John Cage and Karlheinz Stockhausen, asking them to listen for ways the sounds differ from traditional music.

2. Ask students to listen to the audiocassette recording of electronic sounds and study the score for Pinkham's *In the Beginning*. Then ask them to study the score for Rabe's "Rondes." Have them compare how the two scores are notated and identify differences in sound symbols and sound production between the two works.

3. Introduce the term *aleatory,* explaining that this term is applied to music in which certain choices in composition or realization are, to a greater or lesser extent, left to chance or to the whim of the performer. Typical aleatory devices include giving the performer certain responsive choices, such as order of response, dynamics of response, specific length of response, and exact pitch level of response to the notation. Point out that compositions can use varying degrees of "chance" qualities combined with more exacting traditional forms of expression, such as singing, playing, or speaking.

4. Discuss the philosophical idea that some believe that nature and environmental sounds, unaided by human beings, can create beautiful sounds—nature's own music. Have students suggest such sounds (for example, the wind through the leaves, the night song of crickets). Explain that some believe that it is possible to incorporate the free expression of nature into music created by humans.

5. Have students read the text of *In the Beginning*. Then ask them to make musical suggestions of sounds that may be used to represent the text.

6. On electronic keyboards and synthesizers, have students experiment with various sounds that could be used to create a new score for the text of *In the Beginning*. Record segments of students' work.

Indicators of Success

- Experimenting with various sounds, including nontraditional use of traditional instruments and synthesized and electronic instruments, students create a new score for *In the Beginning*.

(continued)

Prior Knowledge and Experiences

- Students have a basic knowledge of synthesizers.

- Some students have intermediate-level keyboard skills, including the awareness of capacities of electronic keyboards.

Follow-up

- At a presentation of students' work, play a recording of *In the Beginning,* and follow it with a performance of the choir's creation.

- Have students create their own aleatory music scores using other texts, such as the following: the American folk song "Cindy," in *Music and You* (New York: Macmillan/McGraw-Hill, 1991), or *World of Music* (Parsippany, NJ: Silver Burdett Ginn, 1991); B. Lloyd Pfautsch's setting of e. e. cummings', "I Thank You God" (New York: Lawson-Gould Music Publishers), 51215; or "Hail Music Fair" by Hans L. Hassler (Westbury, NY: Pro Art), 2139.

- Lead students in an investigation of some of the musical tools of Renaissance composers. Explore questions such as: Why was there so much Renaissance music written for choirs? What kind of instruments did the composers use? Could Renaissance instruments be used in a contemporary aleatory music score?

STANDARD 5A

Reading and notating music: Students read whole, half, quarter, eighth, sixteenth, and dotted notes and rests in 2/4, 3/4, 4/4, 6/8, 3/8, and alla breve meter signatures.

Objective

■ Using rhythm syllables and maintaining a steady pulse, students will chant the recurring rhythm patterns on which a poem set to music is based.

Materials

■ "October's Party" by Elam Sprenkle (New York: Boosey & Hawkes), OCTB6495, two-part, Level 2

■ Chart or transparency of rhythm patterns (see steps 1 and 2)

■ Overhead projector, if transparency is used

Prior Knowledge and Experiences

■ Students are proficient in reading and performing with rhythm syllables quarter, eighth, and sixteenth notes; and dotted quarter- and eighth-note patterns in simple meters.

Procedures

1. While tapping a steady beat, have students chant the following rhythm using any system of rhythm syllables:

[*Note:* Point to the notation on the chart or transparency throughout the Procedures to guide the students' focus.]

2. Have students tap the beat and chant the following rhythm pattern, which you have labeled Rhythm 1:

3. Ask students to tap the beat and echo-chant the text of the first phrase of "October's Party" ("October gave a party, the leaves by hundreds came"), using Rhythm 1. Then have them do the same for the second phrase ("The chestnuts, oaks, and maples, and leaves of every name").

4. Have students echo-chant the text of the third phrase ("The sunshine spread. . ."). Challenge them to decide which part of the notation of Rhythm 1 does not match the spoken text ("sunshine" is even, not dotted). Let a volunteer help you add the corrected notation below Rhythm 1. Label the corrected notation Rhythm 2.

Have students chant the text of the fourth phrase ("Miss Weather. . ."). Ask them whether this text is Rhythm 1 or Rhythm 2. [*Rhythm 1.*] Ask questions that will stimulate discussion about the images that the text suggests so far.

(continued)

5. Ask students to chant the rhythm syllables after you call out which rhythm they should read. Call out the rhythm numbers in the order that they will appear in the score [*1, 1, 2, 1*].

6. Pass out the octavos of "October's Party." Challenge students to discover that voices I and II have identical rhythm. Ask students to speak the text of measures 2–10 of the A section in rhythm. Have students turn to page 7, and help them discover that the same rhythm pattern returns with different text. Invite students to speak the text of measures 26–34 of the A section.

7. Ask students to scan the B section text (measures 16–24) and discuss the imagery of the entire piece. Have students speak the entire text expressively in rhythm.

Indicators of Success

- Students accurately chant the rhythm patterns and identify the difference between the two patterns.

- Students locate familiar rhythm patterns in the score.

Follow-up

- Have students find recurring rhythm patterns in new choral pieces with different meters and use them as markers in reading the score. Ask them to compare recurring patterns to similar but slightly different ones.

- Extend this score-reading approach to finding melodic patterns that are recurring and those that are similar in new pieces.

STANDARD 5B

Reading and notating music: Students read at sight simple melodies in both the treble and bass clefs.

Objective

- Students will identify a familiar song notated in the bass clef and accurately sing a selected phrase with letter names in bass-clef notation.

Materials

- "O Music" by Lowell Mason, arr. Doreen Rao (New York: Boosey & Hawkes), OCTB6352, unison and canon, Level 1—also in *We Will Sing*, by Doreen Rao (New York: Boosey & Hawkes, 1993); or another piece the choir knows well

- Charts or transparencies with notation in both treble and bass clefs for the last phrase of "O Music" (or an easily identifiable phrase from another selected piece)

- Overhead projector, if transparency is used

Prior Knowledge and Experiences

- Students are familiar with treble-clef notation.

- Students can sing from memory "O Music" or the song from which the selected phrase comes.

Procedures

1. Ask students to sing, using solfège or a neutral syllable, the "mystery melody" in treble-clef notation from the chart. Challenge students to identify the melody as the last phrase of "O Music." Then have them sing that phrase with text ("Music, Music, Let the chorus sing").

2. Ask students to stand and sing the entire song with text from memory.

3. Call on a volunteer to identify the starting pitch of the phrase on the chart as G. Then challenge students to sing the entire phrase with letter names.

4. Direct students' attention to the chart with bass-clef notation of the same phrase. Have them identify similarities and differences between this charted phrase and the first one.

5. Pose questions that will help students identify the new melody as the last phrase of "O Music," but in a lower octave. Ask a student to play the new melody in the proper octave from bass-clef notation on the piano. Then ask all students to sing it in a comfortable octave.

6. Ask whether anyone knows the song's starting pitch in the bass-clef notation. Confirm that the starting pitch is G but an octave lower than the starting pitch of the first charted melody. Challenge students to sing the last phrase with bass-clef letter names but in a comfortable octave.

7. Invite students to sing the entire song with text in a comfortable octave.

Indicators of Success

- Students identify the song "O Music" from bass-clef notation of the selected phrase.

- Students accurately sing the selected phrase in bass-clef notation.

Follow-up

- On a regular basis, notate, in treble and bass clef, increasingly longer and more difficult but familiar phrases of songs in the students' repertoire. Have them sing the letter names of these phrases.

STANDARD 5C

Reading and notating music: Students identify and define standard notation symbols for pitch, rhythm, dynamics, tempo, articulation, and expression.

Objective

- Students will connect aural experiences to written symbols by identifying phrases—first by ear; second, from notation on the board; and, third, in their scores.

Materials

- "Carol of the Cuckoo" by Carolyn Jennings (Garland, TX: Choristers Guild), CGA-228, unison, Level 1
- Chalkboard

Prior Knowledge and Experiences

- Students can read and sing simple treble-clef notation.

Procedures

1. Distribute the octavo "The Carol of the Cuckoo" to all students. [*Note*: As you sing the first two verses of the song, the students are not looking at the music.] Instruct students to keep the music closed until you tell them to open it. Ask them to listen for the sound the bird makes as you sing the first verse of the song. When they have found the sound, sing the entire song, asking students to discover how many times the bird says "cuckoo." [*Five times for each of the two verses.*]

2. Ask students, "How are each of the cuckoo calls different from one another?" Then ask them to show with their hands the pitch levels (high, medium, low) of the "cuckoo's" as you sing the song a third time (two verses again).

3. Create three icons to stand for the answer phrases and write them on the chalkboard.

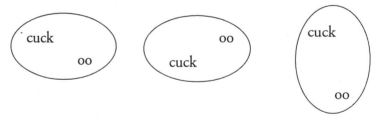

   To allow students to match visual images to their aural experience, ask them to identify the correct order for the "cuckoo" icons. Sing the entire song with the students, having them sing the "cuckoo's" in response to your singing of the question phrases.

4. Ask students to match standard notation for the "cuckoo's," which you put on the board as follows, to the three icons from step 3.

   Sing the song again, having students sing the "cuckoo's" in the correct order from the standard notation on the board.

5. Now ask students to look at the music and sing both phrases of the first two verses.

6. Challenge students to look ahead to see how the rest of the piece compares to the first two verses.

Indicators of Success

- Students correctly identify the icons and standard notation for the "cuckoo" phrases in the first two verses.

- Students find, compare, perform, and discuss differences in the "cuckoo" phrases in the rest of the piece.

Follow-up

- Help students find, focus on, and use identifiable markers of pitch arrangements or rhythm patterns that occur systematically in a new composition. Show students how these markers can make score-reading easier.

STANDARD 5D

Reading and notating music: Students use standard notation to record their musical ideas and the musical ideas of others.

Objective

- Students will create warm-up exercises by filling in (improvising and notating) missing segments of melodies provided by the teacher.

Materials

- Chalkboard, chart, or overhead transparencies with notation for incomplete melodies to be used for warm-ups (see step 1). [*Note*: Select melodies in appropriate tonalities and meters to establish the context for literature the students will be rehearsing and to focus on notational elements in the pieces. You may wish to use simplified notation (just note heads, for example) for initial experiences.]

- Overhead projector, if transparencies are used

- Manuscript paper

Prior Knowledge and Experiences

- Students have listened to and sung songs having major, minor, and modal melody patterns.

- Students have sung from scores having traditional notation.

Procedures

1. Challenge students to sightread the following melody, first silently, then aloud, using any system (solfège, numbers, neutral syllables) of your choice. Assume that a rest fills the missing portion of the melody.

2. Ask students to sing the melody again, improvising silently their own ideas to complete the melody. Repeat this activity.

3. Invite students to sing the melody a third time, improvising aloud their ideas. [*Note:* This step provides low-risk practice, since individuals will not be heard over the din of everyone singing individual ideas at once.] Repeat this activity.

4. Ask a volunteer to sing aloud a solution when the chorus reaches the incomplete portion of the melody.

5. Direct the chorus to sing the melody again, incorporating the volunteer's solution into the missing section.

6. Ask a volunteer to notate the solution on the chalkboard (or, in initial experiences, you notate or have the class help the volunteer notate the solution). Have the chorus sing the melody again. Then have students copy the completed melody onto manuscript paper.

Indicators of Success

- Students improvise missing segments of provided warm-up melodies.

- Students notate their improvisations.

Follow-up

- Provide additional opportunities for singers to improvise and notate melodies or parts of melodies in a variety of styles, such as jazz, gospel, or blues. Over time, students should show an increasing willingness to improvise solutions to musical problems, and their solutions should become more appropriate and musical.

STANDARD 5E

Reading and notating music: Students sightread, accurately and expressively, music with a level of difficulty of 2, on a scale of 1 to 6.

Objective

- Following warm-ups establishing the key of A major, students will sightsing accurately and expressively a two-part piece with a difficulty level of 2.

Materials

- "The Water Is Wide," arr. Luigi Zaninelli (Delaware Water Gap, PA: Shawnee Press), E-83, SA or TB, Level 2

Prior Knowledge and Experiences

- Students can read their own vocal line in a musical score.

- Students have sung music in two parts.

Procedures

1. Lead students in a series of unaccompanied warm-ups of your choice, establishing the key of A major and including prominent patterns from "The Water Is Wide"; for example, *sol-do-re-mi, sol-do-ti-do; do-re-mi-fa-sol, re-do-la-sol.*

2. Ask students to look at page 1 of the score and determine the key. Echo-sing the melodic patterns with the students to reestablish the key of A major.

3. Have students sing through the piece in the following order, encouraging them to maintain good posture and hold their scores so as to be able to follow your conducting:

   a. from rehearsal A to C (verse 1)

   b. from rehearsal E to G (verse 3)

   c. from rehearsal C to E (verse 2)

   d. from beginning to fermata after rehearsal G

   Challenge students to find the patterns from step 1 in these sections and then use them as an aid to sightreading the music.

4. Ask a volunteer from each section to explain how that section will find its pitch after the fermata, and have each section try those strategies. Practice from rehearsal G to H, with sections taking turns singing aloud while others sing silently to foster inner hearing. When each section is secure, have the chorus continue reading in the following sequence:

   a. from rehearsal G to H with all parts aloud

   b. from rehearsal G to end

   c. from beginning to end

   Again, have students identify any occurrences of the familiar pitch patterns before singing.

5. Ask students to sing the piece accurately and expressively from beginning to end.

(continued)

Indicators of Success

- Students find familiar pitch patterns in the context of the song.

- Students perform each verse expressively with few errors in pitch or rhythm.

- Students accurately identify strategies for finding pitches for the coda.

- Students expressively sing a final performance of the piece.

Follow-up

- Ask students to identify familiar pitch patterns such as *sol-do, ti-do,* and *do-la-sol* in other songs as an aid to sightreading new pieces.

STANDARD 6A

Listening to, analyzing, and describing music: Students describe specific music events in a given aural example, using appropriate terminology.

Objective

- Students will identify AABA form of a musical selection they have sung and describe the repetitions and contrasts.

Materials

- "Winter Wonderland," with accompanying recording, in *The Music Connection,* Grade 3 (Parsippany, NJ: Silver Burdett Ginn, 1995); *Share the Music,* Grade 5 (New York: Macmillan/McGraw-Hill, 1995); *Music and You,* Grade 5 (New York: Macmillan/McGraw-Hill, 1991); or *World of Music,* Grades 3 and 6 (Parsippany, NJ: Silver Burdett Ginn, 1991)

- Audio-playback equipment (if recording is used)

- Chalkboard

Prior Knowledge and Experiences

- Students have been learning to sing "Winter Wonderland" in preparation for a concert.

Procedures

1. Invite students to sing or to listen to a recording of "Winter Wonderland."

2. Ask questions that will lead students to discover the form of "Winter Wonderland"; for example, "When does each phrase or section of the music repeat? Are the repeated sections always repeated exactly? Where are the contrasts in each phrase or section?" Label same and different musical ideas as A and B.

3. Diagram the arrangement of the musical ideas on the chalkboard as students identify and describe the form as AABA.

4. Ask students to memorize the music in eight-measure phrases, always being aware of the form. Ask, "Where does the melody repeat? Do the same and different musical ideas make the text more meaningful? How?" Help students to discover any relationship between text and form. Encourage them to tell you what they discover.

Indicators of Success

- Students identify AABA form in a selected piece and demonstrate an increased ability to memorize the piece, based on their study of its form.

Follow-up

- Have students compare the form of "Winter Wonderland" to other songs they have sung or heard.

- Have students identify songs in their repertoire that are in binary, rounded binary, and rondo form, and that are strophic or have da capo sections.

- Have students identify the form of a piece as an aid to expression as well as memorization.

STANDARD 6B

Listening to, analyzing, and describing music: Students analyze the uses of elements of music in aural examples representing diverse genres and cultures.

Objective

- Students will identify uneven meter as characteristic of Serbian folk music by singing, moving, and listening to a gypsy song in 9/8 meter.

Materials

- "Niška Banja" (pronounced "nish-ka bahn-ya"), arr. Nick Page (New York: Boosey & Hawkes), OCTB6517, SAAB or SSAA (can be sung with two, three, or four parts), Level 3

- Recording of "Niška Banja," from *Glen Ellyn Children's Chorus 25th Anniversary Celebration* (available from Glen Ellyn Children's Chorus, 586 Duane St., Ste 102, Glen Ellyn, IL 60137), audiocassette

- Audio-playback equipment

- Globe (or map including Eastern Europe)

Prior Knowledge and Experiences

- As an ensemble, students have sung two- or three-part choral works.

Procedures

1. Establish the uneven 9/8 meter of "Niška Banja" by asking students to clap on 1 as they count aloud 1-2, 1-2, 1-2, 1-2-3; 1-2, 1-2, 1-2, 1-2-3 at an *allegro* tempo until the meter is well established. Then add a step in place, beginning with the left foot on 1 and alternating feet on succeeding 1's as follows:

1-2,	1-2,	1-2,	1-2-3;	1-2,	1-2,	1-2,	1-2-3
L	R	L	R	L	R	L	R

2. Echo-chant the refrain of "Niška Banja" with words in rhythm:

   "Em-kah rahv-la, em-kah-meh rahv-lah,

   An-do nee-shee, nah-meh kahv-lah."

   Echo-sing the melody of the refrain with words and pitches in rhythm.

3. Play the recording of "Niška Banja," and ask students to clap (on 1) the 1-2, 1-2, 1 2, 1-2-3 rhythm every time they hear the refrain on the recording. Play the recording again and have students sing the melody of the refrain every time they hear it. Ask students whether the rhythm of the melody is even or uneven.

4. Distribute the scores of "Niška Banja." Challenge students to locate the refrain in the score. Then ask whether they can find any information in the score that tells them the country from which the song "Niška Banja" comes. [*Serbian gypsy song.*]

5. Ask, "Does anyone know where Serbia is?" [*Eastern Europe.*] Have students locate it on a map or globe.

6. Ask students to give you one typical characteristic of the rhythm of Serbian folk music. [*Uneven.*]

7. Play the piece again, and ask students to sing, move, and clap on the refrain.

Indicators of Success

- Students perform the 9/8 meter of "Niška Banja" and sing the refrain in the correct rhythm.

- After performing and listening to "Niška Banja," students identify uneven meter as a characteristic of this folk music.

Follow-up

- Have students learn the melody parts to the stanzas and at least one harmony part of "Niška Banja." Eventually, teach them as many (up to four) parts as they are capable of learning.

- Have students add "yipping" (flutter top lip with tongue in head voice) as well as tambourine on the strong beats in the instrumental interludes of "Niška Banja."

STANDARD 6C

Listening to, analyzing, and describing music: Students demonstrate knowledge of the basic principles of meter, rhythm, tonality, intervals, chords, and harmonic progressions in their analyses of music.

Objective

- Students will demonstrate perception of the root, third, fifth, and octave of the tonic chord by appropriate movement responses.

Materials

- Songs or recordings of music with prominent use of the tonic chord; for example, "The Star Spangled Banner"; "In the Mood"; "Amazing Grace"; "The Marines' Hymn," in *The Music Connection,* Grade 7 (Parsippany, NJ: Silver Burdett Ginn, 1995) or *World of Music,* Grade 7 (Parsippany, NJ: Silver Burdett Ginn, 1991); "He's Got the Whole World in His Hands"; Johann Sebastian Bach's *Brandenburg Concerto no. 5,* first movement; Joseph Haydn's *Symphony no. 94,* second movement; and "Taps"

- Audio-playback equipment (if recordings are used)

Procedures

1. Play C above middle C on the keyboard and ask students to sing it on the syllable *do.* Tell students to be ready to sing that C (*do*) on cue whenever you conduct it. After talking for a few minutes, give students the cue to sing the C on *do.* Talk for a longer period, and cue the *do* again. Continue to experiment to see how long students can remember *do.*

2. Challenge students to listen carefully as you play the various pitches of the tonic chord. Ask students to respond with the following movements or gestures:

   root—sit or remain sitting

   third—stand

   fifth—stand with arms extended forward, shoulder height

   octave—stand with arms stretched overhead

   fifth below tonic—sit and touch the floor

3. Reinforce each pitch before you add the next pitch, allowing students to experience success before adding a pitch.

4. Play songs or recordings in which the tonic chord is melodically prominent. Challenge students to identify the tonic chord intervals when they hear them in these examples by standing and singing on a neutral syllable or words.

Indicators of Success

- Students identify tonic chord intervals within melodies of music of various styles.

Follow-up

- Help students progress to aural identification of dominant-tonic progression by playing the progression in several keys.

- Play examples of authentic, plagal, and deceptive cadences, and have students identify the authentic cadences.

Prior Knowledge and Experiences

- Students can read standard notation symbols for pitch and rhythm.

- Students have been beginning to work on inner hearing of tonal center and tonic chord intervals.

- Play recorded examples of V-I, such as the coda of Ludwig van Beethoven's *Symphony no. 5,* fourth movement. After students have heard the coda two or three times, ask them to sing *sol* on the root of the dominant chord and *do* on the root of the tonic chord as they listen.

- Ask students to sing "On Top of Old Smoky," in *Share the Music: Songs to Sing and Read* (New York: Macmillan/McGraw-Hill, 1995). Have them indicate by raising their hands which notes of the melody are in the tonic chord.

STANDARD 7A

Evaluating music and music performances: Students develop criteria for evaluating the quality and effectiveness of music performances and compositions and apply the criteria in their personal listening and performing.

Objective

- Students apply evaluative criteria that they have developed to music from their choral repertoire.

Materials

- Student-generated music evaluation form, including lists of adjectives, grouped by categories, that might be used to describe music (copy for each student)
- Repertoire currently being sung in class
- Transparency with copy of student-generated music evaluation form
- Overhead projector

Prior Knowledge and Experiences

- Students have performed a broad repertoire of songs from various style periods.

Procedures

1. Distribute copies of the music evaluation form developed by students previously. Through discussion, review ways to isolate and describe prominent melodic characteristics of a piece of music (for example, wide leaps, minor tonality, pentatonic tonality, or tones that outline chords).

2. Continue with a discussion of ways to isolate and describe prominent rhythmic characteristics of a piece (for example, use of syncopation or rests in unusual places).

3. Ask students to consider the lists of adjectives included with the form. If students have additional suggestions, add words to each group of adjectives.

4. Assign a specific song for the students to use while completing the form. Distribute the music. Let students refer to their music while completing the form. Invite students to sing the song after they have completed the form.

5. Ask students why they like or dislike the song, making sure that they explain their preferences. On the transparency with the evaluation form, generate a collective evaluation form for the selected piece, featuring ideas student volunteers draw from their own evaluation forms.

Indicators of Success

- In applying their evaluative criteria, students identify musical characteristics of selected repertoire.
- Students give reasons for their preferences for the music, based on their understanding of its characteristics.

Follow-up

- Have students, individually or in groups, evaluate a favorite pop song according to the criteria they have developed. Have them justify to the class their reasons for their preferences.

STANDARD 7B

Evaluating music and music performances: Students evaluate the quality and effectiveness of their own and others' performances, compositions, arrangements, and improvisations by applying specific criteria appropriate for the style of the music and offer constructive suggestions for improvement.

Objective

- Students will evaluate the quality of their performance by using an ensemble critique sheet and make suggestions for improving their performance.

Materials

- Ensemble critique sheet (see figure on next page for an example)
- Choral selection that the class knows well
- Audiocassette recorder, microphone, blank tape

Prior Knowledge and Experiences

- Students can perform the selected piece with accurate notes and rhythms.

Procedures

1. Designate for students which measures in the choral selection they will sing as a chorus for evaluation. Also, point out the areas to be evaluated (for example, pitch, phrasing, diction).

2. Distribute the ensemble critique sheet and ask students questions to ensure that they understand the choral vocabulary that is used for evaluation. Be sure that students consider the style of the music in evaluating the areas of performance. (For example, if students were performing "Christmas Lites," arr. David Elliott [New York: Boosey & Hawkes], OCTB6685, three-part treble, Level 3, they would need to consider the performance of "swing eighths" and the long and short sounds of various scat syllables.)

3. Record the chorus as you conduct their singing of the piece. Once the taping is done, ask students to write comments on the form about their section's performance and the ensemble's performance.

4. Lead students in a discussion of their perceptions of the performance before comparing their comments to the actual tape. Check their understanding of vocabulary as they talk about their singing.

5. Once the discussion is complete, play the tape back for the ensemble and, together, compare their initial perceptions to their perceptions in listening to the tape. Help students make additional assessments that may have been revealed by listening to the tape.

6. Ask students to list on the form suggestions for improving their performance. Lead a discussion of these suggestions. Then ask students to sing the selected measures again, incorporating their ideas.

Indicators of Success

- Students critique themselves and others using choral vocabulary.
- Students make suggestions for improvement of their performance and incorporate their ideas into their singing.

Follow-up

- Divide the class into groups. Encourage each group to perform for the rest of the class. Have the class critique the performances with positive comments and suggestions for improvement.

(continued)

ENSEMBLE REHEARSAL CRITIQUE

Name _____

Period _____

Instrument _____

Date _____

Piece _____

3/23/89 version

Write down your critique of the ensemble performance specifying LOCATION [where you performed particularly well or need to improve] and MUSICAL DIMENSIONS [such as rhythm, intonation, tone, balance, articulation, phrasing, interpretation, etc. or any dimension specified by the teacher]. Using words such as "because" be sure to mention any links between your own or your section's performance and the ensemble as a whole. Also include remarks concerning REVISIONS OR PRACTICING STRATEGIES for yourself or the ensemble. Be sure to include the main problem in terms of its dimension and location in the piece you or the ensemble should practice on before or during the next rehearsal.

CRITICAL COMMENTS

Location	Dimension	My (Section's) Performance
		(filled out immediately after performance)

Location	Dimension	Ensemble's Performance
		(filled out after listening to recorded performance)

REVISIONS OR PRACTICE PLANS

For Myself (My Section)

For the Whole Ensemble

ARTS PROPEL assessment form

Specifics ☐ Suggested Revisions ☐ Critical Perspective ☐ ADDITIONAL COMMENTS

USE OTHER SIDE OF PAGE FOR ADDITIONAL COMMENTS

STANDARD 8A

Understanding relationships between music, the other arts, and disciplines outside the arts:
Students compare in two or more arts how the characteristic materials of each art* can be used to transform similar events, scenes, emotions, or ideas into works of art.

Objective

- Students will explore and compare the use of rhythm in music, dance, and theatre.

Materials

- Recording of choice (optional; see step 3)
- Audio-playback equipment, if recording is used

Prior Knowledge and Experiences

- Students have sung simple unison songs as an ensemble and have studied and experienced the concept of rhythm in music.
- Students are proficient with rhythms using whole, half, quarter, eighth, sixteenth, and dotted notes and rests in 2/4, 3/4, 4/4, 6/8, and alla breve meter signatures.

Procedures

1. Lead a discussion about examples of rhythm in nature (repeated patterns that may be seen and, in some cases, heard). Give suggestions, such as horses galloping, the constant change of seasons, or a dripping water faucet. Encourage students to respond with other rhythm patterns found in life. Summarize with a statement about how rhythm influences aspects of living as well as aspects of the related arts.

2. In an echo clapping game using two-, three-, or four-beat measures, review rhythm patterns students have previously learned. After a brief period of demonstrating an exact echo, ask students to create a new rhythmic "answer" to your rhythmic "question." Have students practice as a group, first with multiple answers sounding, and then with individuals responding with an answer. [Rhythm in music]

3. Play a "follow the leader" game similar to the echo game. Lead gestures or traveling movements to an eight-measure pulse that students mimic, using a recording for accompaniment, if you wish. Extend this activity by turning it into a pantomime of a sports situation; for example, baseball, which appeals to many students. Have one group act out the initial routine of a baseball player at bat (the "question"). The second group dramatizes with appropriate actions—the catching of the ball and follow-through (the "answer"). [Rhythm in dance/theatre]

4. Divide the class into groups of five or six students. Have each small group work together for five to eight minutes to create a pantomime of some type of machine; for example, washing machine, sewing machine, or engine that starts (speeds up), runs (repeats), finishes (slows down), and stops (freezes). Have each student represent a necessary part of the machine that reacts to the working of each other part (action and response). Explain to students that they should not talk during the machine's operation, but special sound effects, such as breathing, may be appropriate. Have groups provide an audience for each machine's enactment. [Rhythm in theatre]

(continued)

---

*i.e., sound in music, visual stimuli in visual arts, movement in dance, human interrelationships in theatre.

5. Review, in a discussion format, examples of rhythm in the arts and how they are alike and different.

Indicators of Success

- Students compare the components of rhythm and rhythm patterns in the related arts.

Follow-up

- Have students develop and vary any of the above rhythmic expressions through ornamentation, inversion, timing, and so on to produce a composition.

STANDARD 8B

Understanding relationships between music, the other arts, and disciplines outside the arts:
Students describe ways in which the principles and subject matter of other disciplines
taught in school are interrelated with those of music.

Objective

- Students will identify visually and aurally metrical patterns in lyrics and in music and describe ways that these patterns are related in poetry and music.

Materials

- Metrical index from a hymnbook
- Selected tunes from the hymnbook to match each meter
- Selections from a book of poetry that contains rhyming and rhythmic poems (copies for groups of students; see step 3)
- Selections from a book of folk songs of any genre (copies for groups of students; see step 4)

Prior Knowledge and Experiences

- Students understand and can identify a syllable.
- Students understand the difference between syllabic and nonsyllabic settings of music.

Procedures

1. Using the metrical index from the hymnbook, have students look at the terms (C.M. 8.8.8.8., 8.6.8.6., etc.). Ask them to identify how many syllables are contained in each line of the meter of the selected hymn tunes. Then ask students to identify which of the selected hymn tunes goes with each of the meters.

2. Have students break into small groups for this step and subsequent steps. Ask each group to write up a list matching the meters with the tunes.

3. Using preselected examples from the book of poetry, ask students to identify the meter of various poems. You may want to give different examples to each group.

4. Using preselected examples from the book of folk songs, ask students to identify the meters of various songs. Also ask whether or not the songs are syllabically set.

5. Invite students to find songs that have a meter similar to the selected folk songs, and ask them to determine whether the words are interchangeable.

Indicators of Success

- Students accurately identify and label the metric structure of selected songs and poems.

Follow-up

- Guide students in composing their own melodies for syllabic settings of the common meters.

STANDARD 9A

Understanding music in relation to history and culture: Students describe distinguishing characteristics of representative music genres and styles from a variety of cultures.

Objective

- Students will describe characteristics of jazz swing style and demonstrate them when performing a piece of this genre.

Materials

- "I Don't Know Why," arr. Dave Riley (Van Nuys, CA: Alfred Publishing Company), 7954, SAB, Level 2; 7953, SATB, Level 3
- Jazz recording in slow swing time by the group New York Voices (for example, "Stolen Moments" or "Giant Steps," on *Hearts of Fire,* GRP Records 9653)
- Audio-playback equipment
- Chalkboard

Prior Knowledge and Experiences

- Students have some experience in singing harmony parts.

Procedures

1. Echo-clap a steady beat with emphasis on beats 2 and 4. As the beat continues, whisper a triplet figure such as "she-ke-te." Invite students to join you.

2. Say the words to "I Don't Know Why" in rhythm, and ask students to echo. Direct students' attention to the music, and have them repeat the echo chant as they look at the music.

3. Ask students whether they see any difference in the way the music looks and the way that they are performing. Some students should notice that the rhythm is performed like a triplet even though it is written as two eighth notes. Put the words "straight" and "swing" on the chalkboard. Chant the rhythm both ways, and ask students to tell you which is "straight." Noting that the other rhythm is an example of "swing," ask students to describe one rhythmic characteristic of swing music.

4. Ask students to sing a part of the piece with attention to swing eighths.

5. Play a recording of New York Voices. Have half the students snap on beats 2 and 4. Ask the other half to whisper the triplet "she-ke-te." Ask students to sing a part of "I Don't Know Why," snapping on beats 2 and 4. Play the recording again, and have students listen for accents. Ask students to describe "accent" in swing music.

6. Play the recording of New York Voices once more, directing attention to the way the group sings their tones. [*There is little pitch variation in tone. They start some tones with a feeling of straight tone and add vibrato.*] Challenge students to identify places in the recording where singers slide up to pitches or slide off pitches at the end. Ask them to describe a vocal characteristic of swing music.

7. Invite students to sing "I Don't Know Why," demonstrating jazz tone quality, swing rhythm, indicated falloffs, slides, accents of swing style, and snapping on beats 2 and 4.

Indicators of Success

■ Students describe characteristics of "swing."

■ Students perform "I Don't Know Why" in appropriate jazz swing style.

Follow-up

■ Introduce other jazz pieces written for young voices to add to the group's repertoire—see especially works arranged by David Elliott (New York: Boosey & Hawkes), SSA, Levels 2 and 3.

STANDARD 9B

Understanding music in relation to history and culture: Students classify by genre and style (and, if applicable, by historical period, composer, and title) a varied body of exemplary (that is, high-quality and characteristic) musical works and explain the characteristics that cause each work to be considered exemplary.

Objective

■ Students will describe the characteristics of exemplary Renaissance choral music.

Materials

■ "Da Pacem Domine" by Melchior Franck, arr. Mary Goetze (New York: Boosey & Hawkes), OCTB6187, four-part treble, Level 2

■ Solfège chart of the first twelve measures of "Da Pacem Domine" in all parts

■ Picture of a Renaissance cathedral

■ Recording of a Renaissance piece by a professional choir

■ Audio-playback equipment

Prior Knowledge and Experiences

■ Students have experience singing in harmony parts in a group choral context.

Procedures

1. Ask students with young tenor- or soprano-range voices to sing the first six measures of Part 1a and Part 1b from the solfège chart in the written key. Ask students with young baritone- or alto-range voices to watch the chart and perform the hand signs. Ask baritones to sing measures 7–12 from the solfège chart while tenors do the hand signs.

2. Inquire whether the two parts are exactly the same or different. Help students discover that canons and imitation are characteristic of Renaissance music.

3. Ask students to find in the octavo the first phrase from the chart. When they have found it, ask them to sing it again. Have them find in the octavo the second phrase from the chart. As students sing the first twelve measures of music, ask them to raise their hands when they hear two notes that sound as if they are dissonant or clashing. When students find the spot, ask them to "lean into" the dissonance and sing more lightly when the dissonant tone moves. When the students do this, help them discover the concept of "suspension" by finding the note in a chord that is held over or suspended from the previous chord.

4. Have students sing the two parts together at the place of suspension and lean (physically and vocally) into the suspension and back off at the resolution. Ask the students if there is more interest in the horizontal or vertical movement of the harmony. Guide students to notice the horizontal interest over the vertical interest.

5. Speak the Latin text, emphasizing the stressed syllables, and ask the students to echo. Conduct students in singing the piece with appropriate stress in the text. Ask students whether there is a relationship between text accent and musical accent in Renaissance music.

6. Show a picture of a Renaissance cathedral, and play a recording of a Renaissance piece by a professional choir. Lead students to compare characteristics of Renaissance music heard on the recording to Renaissance characteristics evident in "Da Pacem Domine": imitation, suspensions, more horizontal than vertical interest in harmony, and similarity of musical and textual stress.

7. Ask students to evaluate the stylistic authenticity of their performance of Renaissance music.

Indicators of Success

- Students sing the composition with correct style for the period.
- Students identify characteristics of exemplary Renaissance choral music, such as those found in "Da Pacem Domine."

Follow-up

- Have students listen to recordings of various styles of choral music to discover characteristics of style. Ask them to compare their own performances to models to improve their understanding of those particular choral styles.

STANDARD 9C

Understanding music in relation to history and culture: Students compare, in several cultures of the world, functions music serves, roles of musicians, and conditions under which music is typically performed.

Objective

- Students will perform a South African freedom song with appropriate movement and compare classical choral performances to South African choral singing.

Materials

- "Singabahambayo," from *Two South African Freedom Songs,* arr. Anders Nyberg, ed. Henry Leck (Fort Lauderdale, FL: Plymouth Music Company), WW1240, three-part treble, Level 2
- Conga drum
- *The Power of One* videotape, John G. Avildsen, Warner Home Video 12411
- Videocassette recorder and monitor
- Chalkboard

Prior Knowledge and Experiences

- Students have experience in singing harmony parts in a group choral context.

Procedures

1. Start an easy 1–2 movement, shifting weight between left and right foot. As you shift weight, swivel the heel of the unweighted foot inward. As soon as the students are able, have them join you. Continue to move as you sing the soprano part of the A section of "Singabahambayo." Ask students who can sing in that range to echo. Sing the bottom part of the A section of "Singabahambayo," and ask the students who can sing in that range to echo. Continue the movement throughout the singing.

2. Divide the class into two sections. Invite the sopranos to start. After one repeat, bring in the bottom line. Continue the movement with the singing.

3. Sing the middle part of the A section of "Singabahambayo," and ask students who can sing in that range to echo.

4. Divide the class or chorus into three sections by range. Bring in the soprano part, followed by the bottom part, followed by the middle part. Repeat this process for the B section.

5. Show the portion of *The Power of One* in which the young boy in the video is teaching a song. This is a song of oral tradition, taught part by part. Point out the role of movement in the singing. Ask, "Is the movement merely added to the singing, or do the singing and movement function together in the learning and performance of the song?" Point out that singers should not sing "Singabahambayo" standing in concert formation with hands by the side because movement goes with the singing in African tradition. Also, the song should be sung without accompaniment or with drums. Ask students to join you in singing and moving.

6. As the students recall the video and their singing of "Singabahambayo," ask them to compare South African choral singing with classical choral singing they have experienced; for example, ask what differences there are between learning and performing the music of George Frideric Handel or Wolfgang Amadeus Mozart and the music of South Africa. List the differences on the chalkboard. For example:

Baroque/Classical Choral Music

a. performed in concert

b. taught from written notation

c. performed without intentional movement

d. led by a conductor

South African Choral Music

a. performed informally as a community

b. taught primarily from oral tradition

c. movement is an integral part of performance

d. led by a song leader

7. Lead students in a performance of "Singabahambayo" that includes moving as they sing. Challenge students to experiment with adding a conga drum. Use an easy, slightly syncopated rhythm, such as the following:

Indicators of Success

■ Students describe the manner in which a song such as "Singabahambayo" is typically taught and performed.

■ Students perform "Singabahambayo" and move in South African style as they sing.

■ Students describe differences in the ways classical choral music and South African choral music are taught and performed.

Follow-up

■ Have students view videotapes of other ethnic musics being performed authentically.

■ Expand students' choral repertoire to include pieces from other cultures that require movement or nontraditional ways of using the voice.

RESOURCES

Choral Music Referenced in This Text

"Art Thou Troubled" by George Frideric Handel. Delaware Water Gap, PA: Novello/Shawnee Press. 1038. Unison. Level 1.

"Ave Verum Corpus" by Wolfgang Amadeus Mozart. Chapel Hill, NC: Hinshaw Music. HMC-490. SATB and instrumental parts. Level 2.

"Beautiful Star" by Libby Larson. Boston: E. C. Schirmer. 4202. SACB. Level 2.

"The Birds" by Benjamin Britten. New York: Boosey & Hawkes. OCTB6524. Unison. Level 1.

"Bist du bei mir" by Johann Sebastian Bach. Toronto: Gordon V. Thompson Music. G-183. Unison. Level 1.

"Bye Oh Baby," arr. Malcolm Dalglish. New York: Boosey & Hawkes. OCTB6633. Two-part. Level 2.

"Carol of the Cuckoo" by Carolyn Jennings. Garland, TX: Choristers Guild. CGA-228. Unison. Level 1.

Chichester Psalms by Leonard Bernstein. New York: Boosey & Hawkes. LCB214.

"A Child Is Born," arr. Doreen Rao. For unison voices in canon, unaccompanied. Level 2. In *We Will Sing* (New York: Boosey & Hawkes, 1993).

"Children's Praise" by Ronald Nelson. Garland, TX: Choristers Guild. CGA-5764. Unison. Level 1.

*"Ching-a-Ring Chaw," arr. Aaron Copland. New York: Boosey & Hawkes. OCTB6609. Unison. Level 2.

"Christmas Lites," arr. David Elliott. New York: Boosey & Hawkes. OCTB6685. Three-part treble. Level 3.

"The Cuckoo, the Nightingale, and the Donkey" by Gustav Mahler. New York: Oxford University Press. 82.075. SA. Level 3.

"Da Pacem Domine" by Melchior Franck, arr. Mary Goetze. New York: Boosey & Hawkes. OCTB6187. Four-part treble. Level 2.

"Ding, Dong, Merrily on High," arr. G. A. Smith. Nashville: Broadman Press. 4561-05. SAB. Level 2.

"Dodi Li," arr. Doreen Rao. New York: Boosey & Hawkes. OCTB6679. Unison. Level 1.

"The Dove and the Maple Tree" by Antonin Dvorak. Fort Lauderdale, FL: Walton Music Corporation. WH-141. Two-part. Level 2.

"Feel Good," arr. Barbara Baker and David Elliott. New York: Boosey & Hawkes. OCTB6711. SSA. Level 2.

"The Ferryman" by Dorothy Parke. Toronto: Gordon V. Thompson Music. G-143. Unison. Level 1.

"Freedom Is Coming," collected by Anders Nyberg, ed. Henry Leck. Fort Lauderdale, FL: Walton Music Corporation. WW1149, three-part treble, Level 2. WW1174, SAB, Level 2.

"Friendship Song" (Czech), arr. Doreen Rao. New York: Boosey & Hawkes. OCTB6616. Unison and round. Level 1.

"Gift to Be Simple," arr. M. Pooler. New York: G. Schirmer. 11869. SAT/CB. Level 2.

"Haida" (Hebrew folk song), arr. Henry Leck. Fort Lauderdale, FL: Plymouth Music Company. HL-516. Unison and round. Level 1.

"Hymn to Freedom" by Oscar Peterson. Fort Lauderdale, FL: Walton Music Corporation. WW1135. SSA. Level 3.

"I Don't Know Why," arr. Dave Riley. Van Nuys, CA: Alfred Publishing Company. 7954, SAB, Level 2. 7953, SATB, Level 3.

"In Dulci Jubilo" by Johann Sebastian Bach, arr. Doreen Rao. Unison. Level 1. In *We Will Sing,* by Doreen Rao (New York: Boosey & Hawkes, 1993).

In the Beginning by Daniel Pinkham. Boston: E. C. Schirmer. ECS 2902. SATB. With audiocassette tape of electronic sounds for performance (ECS 2902A). Level 3.

"Jamaican Market Place" by Larry Farrow. Tarzana, CA: Gentry Publications. J62092. SATB. Level 3.

"Jingle Bell Swing," arr. David Elliott. Two-part. Level 2. In *We Will Sing* by Doreen Rao (New York: Boosey & Hawkes, 1993).

"A Jubilant Song" by Allen Pote. Carol Stream, IL: Hope Publishing Company. F979. SACB. Level 2.

*"Jubilate Deo" by Michael Praetorius, arr. Doreen Rao. New York: Boosey & Hawkes. OCTB6350. Unison and round. Level 1.

"Linden Lea" by Ralph Vaughan Williams. New York: Boosey & Hawkes. OCTB6635. Unison. Level 1.

"Mango Walk" (Jamaican folksong), arr. Brent Pierce. Fort Lauderdale, FL: Plymouth Music Company. BP-402. SAB. Level 2.

"Mary Had a Little Blues" by Charles Collins. New York: Boosey & Hawkes. OCTB6758. Two-part. Level 2.

"My Home So Far Away," arr. Lois R. Land, text by Sally Monsour. Alliance Music Publications, PO Box 131977, Houston, TX 77219-1977; telephone 713-868-9980. Two-part. Level 1.

"Niška Banja," arr. Nick Page. New York: Boosey & Hawkes. OCTB6517. SAAB or SSAA. Level 3.

"Nukapianguaq" (Inuit chants), arr. Stephen Hatfield. New York: Boosey & Hawkes. OCTB6700. Four-part (mostly unison/two-part). Level 2.

"O Captain, My Captain" by Elam Sprenkle. New York: Boosey & Hawkes. OCTB6644. SS. Level 3.

"October's Party" by Elam Sprenkle. New York: Boosey & Hawkes. OCTB6495. Two-part. Level 2.

*"Oliver Cromwell," arr. Benjamin Britten. New York: Boosey & Hawkes. OCTB5893. Unison. Level 1.

*"O Music" by Lowell Mason, arr. Doreen Rao. New York: Boosey & Hawkes. OCTB6352. Unison and canon. Level 1.

"Orpheus with His Lute" by Ralph Vaughan Williams. New York: Oxford University Press. OCS52. Unison. Level 1.

*"The Path to the Moon" by Eric H. Thiman. New York: Boosey & Hawkes. OCTB6114. Unison. Level 1.

"The Raggle Taggle Gypsies," arr. Robert Hugh. New York: Boosey & Hawkes. OCTB6747. Two-part treble. Level 2.

"Rondes" by Folke Rabe. Fort Lauderdale, FL: Walton Music Corporation. WH-171. SATB. Level 3.

*"The Sally Gardens," arr. Benjamin Britten. New York: Boosey & Hawkes. OCTB5448. Unison. Level 1.

"She's Like the Swallow," arr. Lori-Anne Doloff. Unison. Level 1. In *We Will Sing* by Doreen Rao (New York: Boosey & Hawkes, 1993).

"Singabahambayo," from *Two South African Freedom Songs,* arr. Anders Nyberg, ed. Henry Leck. Fort Lauderdale, FL: Plymouth Music Company. WW1240. Three-part treble. Level 2.

"Siyahamba," arr. Doreen Rao. New York: Boosey & Hawkes. OCTB6656. Three-part. Level 2.

"Under My Command" by Mary Goetze. New York: Boosey & Hawkes. OCTB6765. Two-part. Level 2.

"The Water Is Wide," arr. Luigi Zaninelli. Delaware Water Gap, PA: Shawnee Press. E-83. SA or TB. Level 2.

"When Cats Run Home" by Eric H. Thiman. New York: Boosey & Hawkes. OCTB5570. Two-part canon. Level 1.

"Where'er You Walk" by George Frideric Handel. Toronto: Gordon V. Thompson Music. VG-197. Unison. Level 1.

* Also in *We Will Sing* by Doreen Rao, listed under "Sources of Songs Referenced in This Text."

Sources of Songs Referenced in This Text

Frey, H., compiler. *Barbershop Memories.* Miami: Warner Bros. Publications, 1984.

Hackett, Patricia, and Carolynn A. Lindeman. *The Musical Classroom: Backgrounds, Models, and Skills for Elementary Teaching,* 4th ed. Englewood Cliffs, NJ: Prentice-Hall, 1997.

Music and You, Grades K–8. New York: Macmillan/McGraw-Hill, 1991.

The Music Connection, Grades K–8. Parsippany, NJ: Silver Burdett Ginn, 1995.

Nash, Grace C. *Music with Children.* Series III, IV and More. Swartwout Productions (703 Manzanita Drive, Sedona, AZ 86336), 1988.

Rao, Doreen. *We Will Sing.* New York: Boosey & Hawkes, 1993. With teacher's kit, including performance portfolio masters and audiocassette.

Round America. New York: Lawson-Gould Music Publishers/G. Schirmer, 1976. LG 51945.

Share the Music, Grades K–8. New York: Macmillan/McGraw-Hill, 1995.

Silverman, arranger. *Folksong Encyclopedia,* Volume 1. Milwaukee: Hal Leonard Corporation, 1981.

Wirth, Marian, Verna Stassevitch, Rita Shotwell, and Patricia Stemmler. *Musical Games, Finger Plays, and Rhythmic Activities for Early Childhood.* Old Tappan, NJ: Prentice-Hall, 1983.

World of Music, Grades K–8. Parsippany, NJ: Silver Burdett Ginn, 1991.

Listening Selections Referenced in This Text

Amabile Youth Singers. Amabile Youth Singers (93 Langarth Street W., London, ON, Canada N6J1P5) IBS 1001. Compact disc.

An Amabile Festival. Amabile Youth Singers (93 Langarth Street W., London, ON, Canada N6J1P5) IBS 1005. Compact disc.

Baroque Duet–Kathleen Battle and Wynton Marsalis. SONY SK46672.

Bernstein, Leonard. *Chichester Psalms.* CBS Records MK 44710.

Britten, Benjamin. *St. Nicholas,* op. 42. Hyperion Records CDA66333.

Fauré, Gabriel. *Requiem,* op. 48. TELARC 80135.

"Freedom Is Coming." Walton Music Corporation WWB528C. Audiocassette.

Glen Ellyn Children's Chorus 25th Anniversary Celebration. Glen Ellyn Children's Chorus (586 Duane St., Suite 102, Glen Ellyn, IL 60137). Audiocassette.

New York Voices. *Hearts of Fire.* GRP Records 9653.

Videotapes Referenced in This Text

Graceland. Paul Simon. Warner Reprise Video 338136.

The Power of One. John G. Avildsen. Warner Home Video 12411.

Additional Resources

ACDA National Committee on Children's Choirs. *ACDA National Directory of Children's Choirs in America.* Lawton, OK: American Choral Directors Association, 1995.

*Anderson, Tom. *Sing Choral Music at Sight.* Reston, VA: Music Educators National Conference, 1992.

The Arts PROPEL Project. Contact Drew Gitomer, Educational Testing Service, Rosedale Road, Trenton, NJ 08541. Also contact Harvard Project Zero, 326 Longfellow Hall, The Harvard Graduate School of Education, 13 Appian Way, Cambridge, MA 02138.

Bartle, Jean Ashworth. *Lifeline for Children's Choir Directors.* Toronto: Gordon V. Thompson Music, 1988.

Caldwell, J. Timothy. *Expressive Singing: Dalcroze Eurythmics for Voice.* Englewood Cliffs: Prentice-Hall, 1995.

Choksy, Lois. *The Kodály Method.* 2d ed. Englewood Cliffs, NJ: Prentice-Hall, 1988.

The Choral Journal, American Choral Directors Association, PO Box 6310, Lawton, OK 73506. Complete issues devoted to children's choirs: March 1989, vol. 29, no. 8; March 1993, vol. 33, no. 8.

Elliott, David. *Music Matters: A New Philosophy of Music Education.* New York: Oxford University Press, 1995.

Hackett, Patricia. *The Melody Book: 300 Selections from the World of Music for Autoharp, Guitar, Piano, Recorder and Voice,* 2d ed. Englewood Cliffs, NJ: Prentice-Hall, 1992.

Hassemann, Frauke, and James Jordan. *Group Vocal Technique.* Chapel Hill, NC: Hinshaw Music.

*Jordanoff, Christine. *Movement in the Middle School Choral Rehearsal.* Children's Festival Chorus of Pittsburgh. Reston, VA: Music Educators National Conference. Videocassette.

*Jordanoff, Christine, and Robert Page. *Choral Triad Video Workshop.* QED Communications. Reston, VA: Music Educators National Conference, 1994. Six-videocassette series and workbook.

Kemp, Helen. *Body, Mind, Spirit, and Voice: Developing the Young Singer.* St. Louis, MO: Concordia Publishing House. Videocassette.

———. *Sing and Rejoice: Guiding Young Singers.* St. Louis, MO: Concordia Publishing House. Videocassette.

———. *Vocal Methods for the Children's Choir.* Philadelphia: Fortress Press, 1965.

McRae, Shirley. *Directing the Children's Choir: A Comprehensive Resource.* Old Tappan, NJ: Schirmer Books/Simon & Schuster, 1991.

*May, William V., and Craig Tolin. *Pronunciation Guide for Choral Literature.* Reston, VA: Music Educators National Conference. 1987.

Moriarty, John. *Diction.* Boston: E. C. Schirmer, 1975.

*Music Educators National Conference. *Teaching Choral Music: A Course of Study.* Reston, VA: MENC, 1991.

Phillips, Kenneth. *Teaching Kids to Sing.* Old Tappan, NJ: Schirmer Books/Simon & Schuster, 1992.

————. *Teaching Kids to Sing.* Old Tappan, NJ: Schirmer Books/Simon & Schuster Macmillan. Six-videocassette series.

Pohjola, Erkki. *The Tapiola Sound.* Fort Lauderdale, FL: Walton Music Corporation, 1993.

Rao, Doreen. *The Art in Choral Music.* Choral Music Experience (CME) Library, volume 3. New York: Boosey & Hawkes, 1990.

————. *The Art Is in Every Child.* Choral Music Experience (CME) Library, volume 2. New York: Boosey & Hawkes, 1988.

————. *Artistry in Music Education.* Choral Music Experience (CME) Library, volume 1. New York: Boosey & Hawkes, 1987.

*————. *Choral Music for Children.* An annotated list. Reston, VA: Music Educators National Conference, 1990.

————. *Teaching Children through Choral Music Experience.* Choral Music Experience (CME) Library, volume 4. New York: Boosey & Hawkes, 1991.

————. *The Young Singing Voice.* Choral Music Experience (CME) Library, volume 5. New York: Boosey & Hawkes, 1987.

Smith, Harvey. *Singing and Growing: Six Video Lessons in Positive Singing Techniques for the Young Student.* Phoenix Boys Choir. Paradise Valley, AZ: Video Teaching Aids.

Telfer, Nancy. *Successful Sight Singing: A Creative, Step by Step Approach.* San Diego: Neil A. Kjos Music Company, 1992.

Webb, Guy., ed., *Up Front: Becoming the Complete Choral Conductor.* Boston: E. C. Schirmer, 1993.

*Available from MENC.

MENC Resources on Music and Arts Education Standards

Aiming for Excellence: The Impact of the Standards Movement on Music Education. 1996. #1012.

Implementing the Arts Education Standards. Set of five brochures: "What School Boards Can Do," "What School Administrators Can Do," "What State Education Agencies Can Do," "What Parents Can Do," "What the Arts Community Can Do." 1994. #4022. Each brochure is also available in packs of 20.

Music for a Sound Education: A Tool Kit for Implementing the Standards. 1994. #1600.

National Standards for Arts Education: What Every Young American Should Know and Be Able to Do in the Arts. 1994. #1605.

Opportunity-to-Learn Standards for Music Instruction: Grades PreK–12. 1994. #1619.

Performance Standards for Music: Strategies and Benchmarks for Assessing Progress Toward the National Standards, Grades PreK–12. 1996. #1633.

Perspectives on Implementation: Arts Education Standards for America's Students. 1994. #1622.

"Prekindergarten Music Education Standards" (brochure). 1995. #4015 (set of 10).

The School Music Program—A New Vision: The K–12 National Standards, PreK Standards, and What They Mean to Music Educators. 1994. #1618.

"Teacher Education for the Arts Disciplines: Issues Raised by the National Standards for Arts Education." 1996. #1609.

Teaching Examples: Ideas for Music Educators. 1994. #1620.

The Vision for Arts Education in the 21st Century. 1994. #1617.

MENC's *Strategies for Teaching* Series

Strategies for Teaching Prekindergarten Music, compiled and edited by Wendy L. Sims. #1644.

Strategies for Teaching K–4 General Music, compiled and edited by Sandra L. Stauffer and Jennifer Davidson. #1645.

Strategies for Teaching Middle-Level General Music, compiled and edited by June M. Hinckley and Suzanne M. Shull. #1646.

Strategies for Teaching High School General Music, compiled and edited by Keith P. Thompson and Gloria J. Kiester. #1647.

Strategies for Teaching Elementary and Middle-Level Chorus, compiled and edited by Ann Roberts Small and Judy K. Bowers. #1648.

Strategies for Teaching High School Chorus, compiled and edited by Randal Swiggum. #1649.

Strategies for Teaching Strings and Orchestra, compiled and edited by Dorothy A. Straub, Louis Bergonzi, and Anne C. Witt. #1652.

Strategies for Teaching Middle-Level and High School Keyboard, compiled and edited by Martha F. Hilley and Tommie Pardue. #1655.

Strategies for Teaching Beginning and Intermediate Band, compiled and edited by Edward J. Kvet and Janet M. Tweed. #1650.

Strategies for Teaching High School Band, compiled and edited by Edward J. Kvet and John E. Williamson. #1651.

Strategies for Teaching Specialized Ensembles, compiled and edited by Robert A. Cutietta. #1653.

Strategies for Teaching Middle-Level and High School Guitar, compiled and edited by William E. Purse, James L. Jordan, and Nancy Marsters. #1654.

Strategies for Teaching: Guide for Music Methods Classes, compiled and edited by Louis O. Hall with Nancy R. Boone, John W. Grashel, and Rosemary C. Watkins. #1656.

For more information on these and other MENC publications, write to or call MENC Publications Sales, 1806 Robert Fulton Drive, Reston, VA 20191-4348; 703-860-4000 or 800-828-0229.